GW00367529

Divers and Diving

Reg Vallintine

Divers and Diving

BLANDFORD PRESS
Poole   Dorset

First published in the U.K. in 1981
Copyright © 1981 Blandford Press Ltd.,
Link House, West Street,
Poole, Dorset. BH15 1LL

British Library Cataloguing in Publication Data

Vallintine, Reginald
  Divers and diving.
  1. Diving, Submarine – History
  I. Title
  627'.72'09   VM977

ISBN 0 7137 0855 7 (Hardback edition)
ISBN 0 7137 1128 0 (Paperback edition)

Phototypeset in Monophoto Apollo by
Asco Trade Typesetting Ltd., Hong Kong

Printed in Hong Kong
by South China Printing Co.

Contents

Acknowledgements

I am greatly indebted to my friends, Don Shiers and Peter Dick for the survey of commercial diving. Peter, who has done considerable research into diving history also checked the first chapter for me. Thanks are also due to Mike Portelly, winner of many international prizes for underwater photography, for the section on this subject. Alan Watkinson, National Diving Officer of the British Sub-Aqua Club and Mike Busuttili, National Training Officer checked the sports diving. Dr David George of the British Museum (Natural History), Colonel Peter Chitty MBE, Officer Commanding the Royal Engineers Diving Establishment, Lieutenant Commander David Bartlett, Diving Training Office, HMS *Vernon* and Chris Apperley of the Cheshire Police provided information for the sections on scientific, military, Royal Navy and police diving. Commander Robinson RN (Retd) was kind enough to check the facts concerning the 'frogmen' and John Towse of the Admiralty Marine Technology Establishment (Physiological Laboratory), supplied information on underwater living experximents. Thanks to Ben Davis and Britton Mockridge of the National Association of Underwater Instructors (Canada), to Peter Stone, editor of 'Dive News' (Australia), to Commander Alan Bax of Fort Bovisand, to Commander 'Jackie' Warner OBE DSC of the Department of Energy and to Mike Borrow of UMEL Limited and John Bevan of Submex for advice and information.Any merit that this book has is due to these gentlemen. The mistakes are my own.

Finally I would like to thank the photographers whose work illustrates this book together with Ley Kenyon, a distinguished diver, author and underwater film maker who provided the paintings of diving old and new; Barry Gregory of Blandford Press who displayed enormous patience in waiting for material that looked as though it would never arrive and my wife, Janie, whose encouragement never flagged inspite of the piles of paper that filled our home.

Reg Vallintine   London   1980

Picture Credits

The colour and black and white artwork was prepared by Ley Kenyon.

Colour photographs taken by Dr. George Benjamin (Pl. 37), Derek Berwin (Pl. 14), Conor Craig (Pl. 36), Jean Deas (Pl. 29), Walter Deas (Pls. 28, 30, 32, 33, 40, 41), Horace Dobbs (Pl. 24), Colin Doeg (Pl. 19), David Doubilet (Pls. 34, 35), Alex Double (Pl. 27), Martyn Farr (Pl. 21), Fort Bovisand (Pls. 52, 53, 54), Jerry Hazzard (Pl. 18), Greg Heythorpe (Pls. 57, 58, 60), Jack McKenney (Pls. 22, 26, 31), Ric Mason (Pl. 38), Keith Muckelroy (Pls. 16, 17), Mike Portelly (Pls. 12, 13, 25), Flip Schulke (Pls. 23, 50, 51), Peter Scoones (Pl. 39), Shiers Diving Contracts Ltd. (Pls. 55, 56). The help of Gillian Lythgoe, Seaphot, is acknowledged.

For black and white photographs, acknowledgement is due to A.M.T.E. (P.L.) (p. 144), Commander D. Bartlett (pp. 130, 132), BBC (p. 110 top right), B. Bitman (p. 111 top right), Diver (p. 139 top right), O. Gugen (p. 111 bottom right), Professor H. Hass (p. 110 top left), the Trustees of the Imperial War Museum (pp. 38, 44), Dr. H. Keller (p. 139 bottom right), S. Maisano (p. 41), Professor J. Piccard (p. 110 bottom left), S. Podell (p. 110 bottom right), Science Museum (p. 25), U.S. Navy (p. 121), M. Ward (p. 147), B. Worth (p. 111 bottom left).

Introduction

Diving and divers have become a part of everyone's world thanks to the television programmes of Hans Hass, Jacques Cousteau and many others, and also to the publicity given to commercial diving off the North Sea oil rigs. Man has been going down undersea for centuries, though, and the art of diving takes many forms and has many purposes. I hope that this short account will provide a background for those who want to know more about who dives or has dived, and why.

Throughout the book I have concentrated on the 'divers' as much as on the 'diving'. There are interesting links between amateur, military and commercial diving through divers who are involved in all three worlds. I have tried to look at the scene from an international point of view although drawing largely on my own experience. Not all underwater activities are covered and the reader will have to look elsewhere for submarines and submersibles. I hope that this book will be of interest not only to those who already dive, but to those who may become divers and to those who will merely watch and read.

There is a widespread feeling that divers dive only for treasure of some sort. This is no longer true in the literal sense. But even the ancient divers were pathfinders and discoverers. Alphonse Esquiros wrote of divers in 1868:

'The desire of knowledge is one great feature which distinguishes modern communities. The sea has no depths, the rocks have no caverns, and the waters have no solitude which can nowadays escape the bold curiosity of man. The diver holds a high place in this brave army of inquirers. Doubtless it is true that it is the desire of riches and the pursuit of his trade which attract him to the bottom of the seas, and not the aspirations of a mind eager for information; but has not this been always the case? Even when he believes that he is acting for his own advantage, and his own advantage only, still it is the Unknown and the Undiscovered that he is pursuing. What was the object of the sanguine adventurers who, with Columbus at their head, launched forth on to the broad Atlantic? They hoped to grasp a visionary prey in the fancy-figured lands floating on the far-distant wave; they looked for gold, but they found a world.'

1
The Earliest Divers

Naked divers and the first bells

All life originated in the sea. Many millions of years ago conditions in the warm, shallow waters formed by centuries of rain pouring on the cooling planet Earth gave rise to simple forms of life. The first of these were single celled amoeba-like globules. More complex forms were slowly evolved and eventually primitive fish developed. They had soft cartilage instead of bones and were the ancestors of our present day sharks, skates and rays. Through their bodies circulated the water of the ancient seas, their gills extracting the life-giving oxygen.

Eventually one of these marine creatures flopped out on to the land – probably chased there by a large predator. The species slowly developed lungs instead of gills and the upward progress to man had really begun. These animals still carried the remains of the sea in their bodies as blood. Even today, in emergency, salt water can be used to replace blood to keep their human descendants alive.

William Beebe, the distinguished biologist and underwater explorer, pointed out that the sea has become gradually saltier every year as the rivers of the world wash thousands of tons of salt and other materials into it, while the salinity of our blood has remained the same. The sea is now three times saltier than the remains of it in our bodies. If we can calculate back and find the time when the ocean was only a third as salty we will find the date when our first ancestors crawled out on land!

At the British Sub-Aqua Club 'Brighton Conference' in 1960 Professor Sir Alister Hardy first introduced his theory of 'aquatic man'. He suggested that there were many human features which indicated that there was a period when man, perhaps short of food, went back into the sea to find it. He pointed out that man alone among the non-aquatic mammals, can swim effectively underwater and that babies make involuntary swimming movements. The hair tracts on the human body point towards the middle of the back for streamlining and we have a layer of blubber not found on the apes. If man had walked into the shallow seas he might, postulated Hardy, have lost most of the hair on his body – except the head and quickly adopted an upright posture.

Certainly human hands are adapted for manipulation not loco-motion and perhaps they had developed while primitive man grubbed on the bottom for shells and edible growths. It is certainly true that early man sought food in the sea. Piles of shells are found in the remains of early settlements and seafood was probably used to supplement the diet. Later, in Palaeolithic times man was harpooning fish in the clear waters of the Mediterranean as shown by drawings of fish and by other evidence. In the area that is now Denmark early man lived on oysters, mussels, cockles, plus cod and sole which he could harpoon in a few feet of water.

Some of the earliest records of divers date from 4500 B.C. in Mesopotamia. In 3200 B.C., carved ornaments from Thebes incorpo-rated mother-of-pearl which can only have been obtained in quantity by diving for the shells that provide it. Chinese divers were bringing up pearls for their Emperor in 2250 B.C.

Homer, writing perhaps as early as 1000 B.C. refers to the extensive use of sponges. Fishermen who became sponge divers had to go down deeper than 22m (70ft) to get the best specimens. Another writer tells us that, 'They dared not allow their keen and far-seeing eyes to be dimmed by the use of wine'! The method described was for the diver to go down weighted by a rock and connected to the surface by a line. He took oil into his mouth, poured it into his ears and then covered them with oil-soaked sponges. Ignoring the pain in his ears he hit the bottom, spat out some oil and began to cut the sponges with a sharp knife. A tug on the line was his signal to be pulled to the surface.

The British Museum has a frescoe dating from 900 B.C. which allegedly shows that the Assyrians were underwater swimmers. They breathed air from goatskins but would have needed a 22kg (50lb) weight belt to sink!

The story of Glaucus, the diver-fisherman from Anthedon where all the men, women and children were famous for their diving, is well known. In the fourth century B.C. Dicaearchus of Messene, a pupil of Aristotle, wrote of them; 'They are of reddish complexion and quite emaciated and the tips of their nails are worn away by their work in the sea'.

Soon breath-hold divers were going deeper for Mediterranean red coral, a more valuable commodity than sponges. Further afield in the Red Sea and the Persian Gulf they recovered pearls and by 550 B.C. this industry had spread to India and Ceylon. Oppian describes the sport of underwater hunting, mentioning the characteristics of different Mediterranean fish such as the 'Sar' or sea bream.

The most famous ancient diving team was undoubtedly Scyllias and his daughter, Cyana. During the Median wars of the fifth century B.C. Scyllias was engaged by the Persian King, Xerxes, to bring up sunken treasure. He did this successfully but the king refused to let him return to Greece. Scyllias successfully made his escape and then taught his daughter to dive using a breathing tube. 'One day they saw the fleet of Xerxes riding at anchor ... but being buffeted by a terrible storm. The father and daughter plunged into the sea and cast off the anchors of the Persian ships causing a great disaster. From this' the ancient writer concludes, 'we can at least be sure that young women may dive into the sea without fear of losing their virginity.' This encouraging statement is doubtless referring to the fear that the water pressure that broke the eardrums might have had a similar effect on other membranes! Scyllias and Cyana had statues erected in their honour at Delphi.

Greek mythology has many references to underwater activities. Aristotle, the first great naturalist, writes so accurately about fishes that you begin to think he was a diver. Apart from sponges, other products used by the ancient Greeks, such as the imperial purple dye from the *Murex* shell, could only have been obtained by diving.

It was Aristotle who was the first to describe a diving bell in which Alexander the Great was supposed to have gone down in 332 B.C. He peered out at underwater sheep and dogs and a great creature that took three days to pass! Alexander also used divers successfully during the siege of Tyre.

Aristotle also describes diving bells used by sponge divers. Originally these were merely large open inverted cup-shaped containers that trapped air inside when they were lowered into the sea. The air was pressurised by the water trying to force its way in. The divers could exist for quite long periods in the bell and even make brief sorties outside.

About this time too the first 'demolition frogmen' appeared during the wars between Greece and Sparta in the fifth century B.C. when the Spartans were besieged on an island and were supplied with food by divers. Later stakes were driven into a fairway to make it impossible for Athenian ships to enter. The 'frogmen' successfully sawed through them. In the Levant, divers made a profitable business of recovering valuables from wrecks. They received a percentage of the value depending on the depth of the wreck. The Japanese 'Amas', girl divers, have been going down since before the birth of Christ gathering pearl oysters, shellfish and edible seaweed. The first

11

representation of diving goggles was found on a Peruvian vase dating from the second century and free diving was carried out in the New World before Columbus by North American Indians, Mayans and the Yahgan Indian women of Tierra del Fuego.

The first diving 'machines'

The barbarian invasions of Europe slowed down the development of the art there but in the year 934 A.D. the Arab geographer Mas'udi wrote of the pearl and coral divers. In the year 1000 the King of Sweden sent one of his lieutenants, Eric the Eloquent, to destroy the infamous Danish pirate called Oddo. During the night Eric sent divers underwater to drill holes in all of Oddo's ships. The following morning they began to list and Eric attacked and killed all the distracted pirates.

The most famous Arab diver was born in Egypt and was known as Ahsan-ul-Ghawasin or Issa. He served in the fleets of Saladin and was the only survivor of his side in a sea battle that took place on 6 August 1190. He escaped by swimming underwater from the Christian archers. During the Third Crusade the city of Acre was besieged by sea and Issa is reputed to have constructed a 'little breathing machine' which included a bellows and a heavy stone on a belt which allowed him to stay just below the surface. He successfully swam ashore carrying money and letters but each time was horrified to see the bodies of his compatriots who had been killed by attackers decomposing on the bottom where they were eaten by conger eels, octopi and crabs. Issa was eventually seen, followed by boats and killed by a crusader's arrow.

Another famous eleventh century diver was Nicholas Pesce or 'Nicholas the Fish'. Nicholas was an expert swimmer who was reported to have carried letters from the King of Sicily from Sicily to Calabria in Italy. The king offered him a golden cup to dive into the whirlpool of Charybdis, a feat that he successfully accomplished. His stories of the life on the bottom so interested the king that he promised more gold for a further report. The second time was too much and 'Nicholas the Fish' never reappeared at the surface.

More underwater sabotage took place in 1203 when a skilled diver called Gauberte carried combustible materials underwater to the Island of Andelys, which was being attacked by King Philip Augustus, and burned down the defences.

In 1331 pearl divers were operating in large numbers in the Persian Gulf using breath-holding techniques and goggles made of tortoiseshell. In 1421 a Genoese diver with only a pair of pincers cut all

Issa, the most famous Arab diver of the ancient world. He served with the navy of Saladin during the Third Crusade in the 12th century.

the anchor cables of the fleet of the King of Aragon at Bonifacio and caused the defeat of the Spaniards.

Columbus discovered a pearl diving industry flourishing on the coast of Venezuela in 1498 and on his return to Spain the king ordered the establishment of a pearl fishing centre. The industry has thrived at Cubagua in Venezuela ever since. Later the Spaniards made use of the Lucayan Indians of the Bahamas who would descend to nearly 30m (100ft) holding large stones in their arms and jumping overboard with only a net bag about their necks.

During the Middle Ages the same methods were used as those that had been successful since ancient times – the free diver, the breathing tube and the diving bell. With the Renaissance came new inventors designing devices that would allow men to walk and move on the bottom. Most of these were impracticable due to lack of knowledge of the laws of pressure involved. A flood of new ideas was recorded in

13

the notebooks of Leonardo da Vinci. These even included primitive goggles and fins. In a book published early in the sixteenth century, Vegetius illustrated three types of suit intended to allow a diver to walk on the bottom. Like earlier drawings they mostly involved long simple tubes to the surface and would not have worked as the water pressure on the diver's chest would have prevented air from being drawn down more than 45cm (18in) or so.

Diving bells were forging ahead, however, and in 1531 the earliest dependable record of one in actual use was published. The bell was made by Lorena and was used in an attempt to raise Caligula's pleasure galleys sunk in Lake Nemi in Italy. This small bell contained the top half of a man's body and fitted over the diver's shoulders. It had a glass window and the user's hands could be extended under the rim.

A German author, Tassinier, describes in some detail the descent of two Greek divers into the River Tagus at Toledo which was also watched by the Emperor Charles V and ten thousand people. The bell was described as 'a very large vase hanging mouth downwards suported by ropes from above'. The divers sat on planks inside holding lighted candles. They came out with them still burning. It was harder to work underwater, however. Men certainly did so using the smaller bells in which legs and arms could be in the water while their heads could be kept above. They even left the bell for short periods, holding their breath. Although bells were frequently used, few understood the principles involved until George Sinclair, a professor at Glasgow University, put forward a coherent theory on the subject in 1669. He also described the recovery of cannons from the Tobermory galleon in 1665, the first use of a bell in British waters. One of the most successful treasure hunters was William Phipps who used a bell to recover treasure from a Spanish galleon sunk in the West Indies. Later in 1685 using breath-holding pearl divers he located and salvaged the wreck of the Spanish galleon *Almiranta* and its cargo worth £1$\frac{1}{2}$ million in today's prices. Phipps was knighted by King James II for his successful salvage.

Meanwhile combat swimmers were still active and during the siege of Malta in 1565 the Turks used divers to destroy a pallisade erected by the defenders. They were attacked by Maltese divers and a 'terrible battle' ensued on the bottom.

Throughout the history of diving there are records of men lying just under the surface breathing through hollow reeds to escape detection by enemies and this quite probably did happen. It is recorded that cossacks in the seventeenth century lay all day in the

Black Sea to escape the 'galleys of their masters.'

Gradually the importance of the laws of pressure to diving was realised. In 1681 a priest, Abbé Jean de Hautefeuille in *The Art of Breathing Underwater* explains that: 'It is not possible for man to breathe air at normal atmospheric pressure when he is himself under water at depth'. Some years before an Englishman, Robert Boyle, had formulated the law named after him which was to revolutionise the concept of diving. Boyle also built a pressure chamber to study animals and was the first to see a tiny bubble form in the eye of a decompressed viper. This was the effect of 'the bends', a condition which was to cripple and kill divers for centuries to come.

One of the best known and most successful diving bells was that of the famous astronomer Edmund Halley. Halley was secretary of the Royal Society and published his, *Art of Living Underwater* in the *Philosophical Transactions* of the Society in 1716. Halley understood many of the problems of pressure underwater. His bell was constructed of wood coated with lead and was refuelled with two barrels of about 160 litres (36 gallons) each which were sent down to it where the divers could turn a tap to allow the air from the barrels to refresh them. Divers also worked away from the bell for short periods, securing cannon and other items to be lifted. He descended with his bell in 1690 to a depth of 18m (60ft) and stayed for 90 minutes. Soon after this a French professor of mathematics, Denis Papin, suggested that diving bells should be supplied with fresh air continuously using tubes and powerful bellows or pressure pumps. Halley's bell was heavy and difficult to maintain and in the following years lightweight and cheaper alternatives were developed. These included Martin Treiwald's bell. Treiwald, an officer in the Swedish army, produced his bell in 1728 and it continued to be used in Sweden during the greater part of the eighteenth century.

In 1775 Charles Spalding of Edinburgh produced an improved bell which could be raised and lowered by the occupants. This was achieved by the use of ballast resting on the bottom and attached to the bell by a tackle whose length could be regulated by those inside. Spalding's bell was one of the safest and most successful, however both he and his son were killed during a dive in 1783. The first really modern bell was developed by John Smeaton, builder of one of the Eddystone lighthouses. He designed it in 1788 and it was used in the building of Ramsgate Harbour in 1790. The bell was of cast iron and at last a sufficient supply of air was delivered by a force pump. An air reservoir was provided, as were non-return valves to prevent air being sucked out of the tube. This bell was further developed by the engineer James Rennie who mounted it on rails on the bottom to enable easy movement. A Captain Dickinson raised £370,000 of treasure from the sunken frigate *Thetis* off Cape Frio in Brazil in 1831 using 'home made' diving bells. By the end of the eighteenth century most large ports had their own diving bells used for construction, repairs and salvage.

At the time that Halley was developing the modern bell another highly original and, above all, successful answer to the breathing problem was provided by an Englishman from Devon who was finding difficulty in supporting his large family. John Lethbridge decided that the diver could be protected from pressure by putting him in a resistant tube which left his bands free for working. His 'engine' was constructed by a London cooper. Lethbridge wrote that it was, 'made of wainscot, perfectly round, about 6 feet in length, about $2\frac{1}{2}$ feet in diameter at the head and about 18 inches in diameter at the foot and hooped with iron hoops without and within'. In metric terms this gives a device about 1.85m long, 76cm in diameter at one end and 46cm at the other. On the bottom was a glass port 10cm (4in) in diameter and 3.2cm ($1\frac{1}{4}$in) thick. The diver was lowered in the tube in a horizontal position and his arms emerged through two specially constructed holes. From time to time his tenders hauled the 'hogshead' to the surface, opened the air holes and renewed the air with a pair of bellows. Lethbridge explained, 'I lie straight upon my breast all the time I am in the engine which hath many times been more than six hours, being frequently refreshed upon the surface by a pair of bellows. I have stayed, many times thirty-four minutes. I have been ten fathoms deep many more than a hundred times and have been to depths of twelve fathoms, but with great difficulty'. The 'difficulty' was almost certainly due to the pressure of the water on Lethbridge's unprotected arms.

The importance of Lethbridge's story is that his apparatus actually worked and thus fulfilled his dream of recovering treasure from wrecks. He travelled the world in search of salvage. He was contracted by the Dutch East India Company and salvaged the wreck of the *Slot ter Hoogte* making a profit of 265,000 guilders for the company. In January 1728 be was known to be working with his son on a wreck in Table Bay, South Africa. His first dive had been in 1715 and he seems to have continued diving happily for at least thirty years. He is undoubtedly the most important forerunner of the modern working diver.

In 1750 Captain Jacob Rowe produced a diving engine similar to Lethbridge's but in the shape of a 'Scotch snuff mill'. A number of

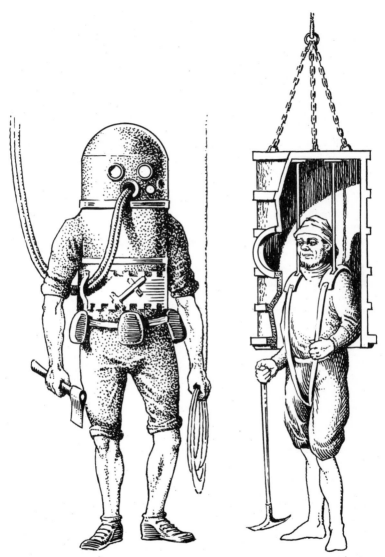

Klingert's diving apparatus (left) was demonstrated in the River Oder in 1789. In 1531 Lorena's one-man diving bell (right) was used successfully on Roman galleys in Lake Nemi.

inventions and developments quickly followed. In 1754 divers were succesfully salvaging a man-of-war off the Needles, Isle of Wight, using apparatus based on the Vegetius model. It seems to have consisted of a brass helmet and a leather dress. In 1771 a Frenchman, Freminet, produced a simple helmet with eye holes. He called it the 'hydrostatergatic machine' as it allowed man to live and move underwater! Its chief defect was the small reserve of air taken below. Many still did not understand the effect of water pressure and in 1774 a bizarre record attempt was made by John Day in Plymouth Sound. He sank himself inside a reinforced box to 43m (140ft) but never returned. Freminet's suit was further developed with a tube to the surface and a bellows. He apparently used it without mishap to 15m (50ft) for an hour.

In 1786 two Englishmen, John and William Braithwaite, were recovering guns sunk off Gibraltar using their own design of helmet. They also successfully salvaged silver dollars from a wreck off the Cape Verde Islands in 1790. In 1806 they recovered part of the wreck of the *Earl of Abergavenny* from a depth of 18m (60ft) together with £75,000 in dollars. In 1797 a German called Klingert produced a somewhat similar device with a cylindrical hood made of strong tin plate worn with a leather jacket and 'drawers'. On 24 June 1798 a man called Joachim dived into the River Oder using the apparatus and proved its practicability by sawing through the trunk of a large tree. Again the pressure against the unprotected arms and legs must have been painful at depth.

William Forder produced a device with a copper casing for the upper half of the body in 1802. It is doubtful whether the air that was supplied by bellows from the surface would have been sufficient. James Fullarton and Frederic Drieberg also produced interesting but hardly practical variations on the theme.

Helmet divers of the Nineteenth Century

John Deane and the first helmet
The stage was now set for the biggest development since Lethbridge. It was an invention that was to be so important and successful that it would become the standard method of diving for the next 150 years.

The story of the creation of the standard diving helmet and suit was not well known until Alexander McKee, researching the early work on the wreck of the *Mary Rose* came upon a number of accounts which conflicted with the 'standard version' of the histories. He describes the detective work in his book *History Under the Sea*.

The invention of the helmet as we know it today could be said to have begun in a burning farm near Whitstable in Kent in about 1820. The stables were alight and a team of horses were trapped inside. Dense smoke kept rescuers away and the only water pump threw a small jet which had little effect. In the watching crowd was a powerfully built local man, John Deane, who thought of a plan. He borrowed a helmet which was part of a suit of armour in the hall of the farmhouse, placed it over his head, secured the pipe from the pump and asked that the air be pumped through slowly. He walked into the stables through the dense smoke and brought out one horse after another until they were all saved.

John Deane's brother, Charles, patented the idea for fire fighting in 1823 but John had other ideas. He rigged up his helmet with two large round windows and a watertight dress. He walked into the sea at high water on a calm day but found that when the water covered his head the air inflated the suit and he turned upside down. He quickly invented lead-soled boots! He worked with the 'sweepers' who dragged for lost anchors in the area. When they snagged one, he went down in his suit and made it fast to a chain. He advanced to wreck diving and worked on the wreck of the *Royal George* that had been sunk in Spithead in 1782. By this time he had developed a watertight rubber dress and a helmet large enough for him to turn his head inside. It now had three glass face plates and a flexible rubber tube to the pump on the surface.

Deane produced a handbook for the apparatus in 1836 in which he writes: 'A safe and effectual method of descending into great depths of water appears to have been unknown, or but very imperfectly developed, until the introduction of that well-known diving apparatus invented by myself and my brother. The invention, after a long series of experiments, vast study and labour, was brought to full perfection in 1828'. This judgement was substantiated by others writing in 1840 and a detailed description of the apparatus was given by Colonel Charles Pasley of the Corps of Royal Sappers and Miners (later to be the Royal Engineers) who carried out extensive diving operations on the *Royal George* in the 1840s.

Other types of helmet were also appearing in the 1830s. They included those of Bethell, Fraser and Siebe. Deane's original suit came up to his chin and the helmet merely rested on the diver's shoulders. Air escaped around the bottom of the helmet which acted like a miniature diving bell. Both Bethell and Fraser patented their suits in 1835 and these may have been the first enclosed diving dresses. The helmets were joined to the suit so that the diver did not have to stand upright or risk water getting into the helmet. Augustus Siebe, a German-born instrument maker and the founder of the firm Siebe Gorman, became acquainted with the Deanes and improved on their original design. It seems probable that Charles Deane sold the 'rights' to Siebe and the design then became known as Siebe's. Certainly Seibe's improvements, not only to the suit, but also to the pump ensured the continuance of the method as the most efficient one for the nineteenth century.

The Deanes went into business as 'salvage engineers', spending many hours on the bottom and diving from a fishing smack, the *Mary*, owned by their partner, William Edwards, and charged five guineas a day! They dived on the wreck of the *Mary Rose*, sunk in 1545 and now the most famous wreck in British waters, and arranged for their finds to be carefully recorded and painted. John Deane later laid the piles for the Houses of Parliament. He was born in 1800 and was still diving in 1856, under the ice in the Crimea to salvage sunken Russian warships!

Colonel Pasley and the Royal George

The art of diving demolition and salvage really began in 1839 at Spithead on the wreck of the *Royal George*. She had sunk with 1300 people on board including 250 visiting women and children. She was being heeled to repair a pipe when a lighter began to offload rum onto the side already low in the water. Her ports went under and she sank in 20m (65ft) of water with the tops of her masts still above the surface. The wreck was a danger to shipping and attempts to raise her were ineffective. In 1839 Colonel Charles Pasley, a remarkable engineer, arrived with four other officers, 23 sappers and nine men. These soldiers carried out the first large scale salvage operation and founded the first navy diving school. Pasley looked at the various helmets and adopted the version of the Deanes' that had been improved by Siebe by being sealed to a watertight suit. The divers worked in pairs, creating one of the first rules of underwater safety. They had to demolish the wreck with gunpowder and recover the cannons and brass fittings.

Colonel Pasley used oaken hogsheads, sheathed in lead, for the demolition. The divers placed them against the wreck before being hauled up. A wire ran from the barrel to a battery on deck and this was used to explode the charge. On deck they filled the barrel with gunpowder and welded it shut. This risky procedure was carried out by a private soldier who had never before welded anything in his life!

The best divers were Sergeant Harris and Lance Corporal Jones.

Pasley encouraged competition for the biggest sling loads recovered and the soldiers revelled in the attentions of the numerous press correspondents on board. Trying one day to better the efforts of the others, Corporal Jones slung five heavy 'pigs' of iron ballast. To tighten his sling he climbed on top of the load and jumped up and down in his lead-lined boots. The load swung under him, fouling his air pipe and safety line and twisting them around the chain. He was hopelessly entangled with his air line cut off 18m (60ft) below the surface. Jones leaned back and slashed off his pipe and line with his knife. He kicked off his weighted boots and floated to the surface using his bands as hydrofoils and exhaling continuously. This seems to have been the first successful emergency ascent in which the diver knew how to prevent his lungs from bursting as the compressed air inside expanded with the decreasing surrounding pressure.

The first medical record of the diver's 'squeeze' was made on their salvage operation. This horrible accident can happen to helmet divers if their air pipe ruptures or they fall into greater depths before they can adjust the air pressure in their helmets. In the worst cases the flesh is sucked off up the pipe with the sudden release of pressure caused by a severed pipe and the rest of the unfortunate diver's body is forced into the helmet. When Private John Williams' pipe broke on the *Royal George* be felt 'a sudden shock and a tremendous pressure'. His tender hauled him in quickly and he survived, although his face and neck were swollen and livid, his eyeball capilliaries ruptured and the blood was flowing from his ears and mouth. He spent a month in hospital and recovered but was unable to dive again.

Corporal Jones' record lifts were challenged by a hulking Private Girvan from Scotland. One day they grabbed opposite ends of a balk of timber on the wreck. Jones tied on his rope and Girvan attacked him! Jones decided not to fight with the furious soldier and started climbing the rope. Girvan grabbed for his legs. Jones kicked out to free himself and put his metal tipped boot through Girvan's face plate. The tenders began to haul up when they saw the thrashing lines. Jones was clinging to the distressed man and Girvan arrived alive. They shook hands and thereafter formed an unbeatable team.

The salvage went on for four seasons. In 1840 further improvements were made to the diving apparatus at Deane's suggestion. Sailors from the navy began to envy the soldiers whose undersea exploits were regularly reported in the press. Pasley brought 13 petty officers and men from the HMS *Excellent* and set up the first Royal Navy diving school under Jones. They demolished the wreck of HMS *Edgar*. The only time that Jones was worried was when he was diving in very low visibility and came across a smooth soft object on the seabed. He felt a sort of grating along its length and suddenly froze. He was feeling the vertebrae of a human body! He went up the ladder like a flash and got another diver to remove the corpse.

Colonel Palsey reported, 'Whatever success has attended our operations is chiefly attributed to the exertions of Corporal Jones, of whom as a diver I can not speak too highly'.

Helmet Dives and Divers
A notable trial of the various types of diving helmets was held in 1855 at the Paris International Exhibition. The British Heinke model was judged the best and received a First Class Medal.

In the middle years of the nineteenth century, salvage divers used to gather at Whitstable. When a ship went down the agents took a train from London and went round the public houses recruiting divers. A good diver earned a pound a day. John Deane's 'ordinary' was the main diver's pub in Whitstable. During the building of the Westminster Bridge in the 1860's there was considerable work for divers and the Whitstable men came up to London and used a pub in Lower Marsh Street, Lambeth which became known as 'The Diver's Arms'.

The exploits of divers made headlines in the nineteenth century. One of the most famous divers was Alexander Lambert who was built like a heavyweight boxer and went where the jobs were toughest. In 1880 a tunnel that was being excavated under the River Severn in Gloucestershire became flooded. It could not be pumped out unless a heavy iron door deep inside was closed. It was inaccessible to a helmet diver trailing air hose and lines as it would be neccessary to go 60m (200ft) down a vertical shaft and then 300m (1000ft) along the tunnel. The new autonomous oxygen 'lung' had just been invented by Henry Fleuss and he offered it to Lambert for the job. No one knew that oxygen could be poisonous at depths greater than 9m (30ft). Lambert dropped into the black pit and groped his way along the tunnel, working his way along the builders' railway lines in complete darkness. He found the door, put his back to it, and heaved. It was wedged – the rails were running over the sill. He ripped one up with his bare bands and the other would not budge so he plodded back to the shaft, climbed up for a wrecking bar, went back, forced the second rail up and slammed the door shut.

Three years later the tunnel flooded again. He went back with the oxygen lung but this time he nearly died of oxygen poisoning. After a good night's sleep he called for his trusty helmet and dress. Two divers paid out his lines from the bottom of the shaft as he marched into the tunnel weighed down by boots, breast weight and helmet and dragging his lines. He slammed the door again.

There was little that bothered Lambert. Sir Robert Davis who had met Lambert as a boy was still Chairman of Siebe Gorman and Co. in the 1950's and told the story that once Lambert was coppering the bottom of a coaling ship at Diego Garcia in the Indian Ocean. A nosy shark hung round day after day and irritated the great man. Finally Lambert held up his bare band as bait and lured it in to close range. He lunged with his diver's knife and ripped into its skin. Then he calmly fixed the shot rope to its tail and signalled for it to be hauled up! In 1885 Lambert, single handed, recovered £180,000 of gold bullion from the wreck of the *Alphonse XII* sunk in 50m (162ft) of water off Grand Canary, but he got a bad attack of the 'bends' and had to retire.

Decompression Sickness
Robert Boyle had first discovered decompression sickness or 'bends', as it came to be known, in 1660, but it was 200 years before a French scientist, Paul Bert, really explained what it was. Bert, born in 1833, was a physiologist and champion of women's rights. He was also a lawyer, a doctor and a biologist! His masterwork, *La Pression Barometrique* was published in 1878, and drew on the experience of a young doctor, Gall, who had dived with sponge divers and recorded their symptoms. Bert's most important discovery was of the importance of nitrogen breathed under pressure. 79% of our atmospheric air is nitrogen, and when compressed air was used to prevent the diver from being squeezed, Bert discovered that it began to dissolve in the fatty tissues. The problem came when the diver returned. If he came up too quickly the excess nitrogen formed bubbles which could damage the nervous system and block the circulation of the blood. Bert's answer was to raise the diver very slowly so that the nitrogen would gradually escape through his system as he breathed and, if the bubbles had already formed, to 'recompress' the diver in an air chamber to force them back into solution.

The full application of these discoveries had to wait until 1896 when a craggy Scot, John Scott Haldane, carried out a long series of experiments with the Royal Navy which resulted in the first practical 'decompression tables'. Bert had shown that a man could be drawn up quickly from a depth of 10m (33ft) without suffering from 'bends' and Haldane postulated that the trick was to halve the pressure. 'Therefore I can haul a man from six atmospheres to three'. He would

23

stop the man thereafter to spend a certain time at a set shallow depth to pass off the excess nitrogen. Haldane produced tables for depths down to 60m (200ft), double the previous range of diving. He and his team tried them out first. Lieutenant Damant successfully dived to 64m (210ft) proving the new tables. Haldane published his report for six pence in 1907. His results formed the basis for the diving tables of all the world's navies.

The United States Navy now took up the research and in 1914 reached a new record depth of 83.5m (274ft) in the open ocean. In 1915 the US submarine F-4 sank in 93m (304ft) of water and was reached by Navy diver Frank Crilley. This was close to the limit of compressed air diving.

One of the most remarkable salvage operations was the recovery of £12 million worth of bullion from the wreck of the *Laurentic*, a white star liner that had been sunk by the Germans in 1917. Captain G.C.C. Damant and his team of Royal Navy divers worked under 'impossible' conditions in the crumbling wreck 40m (132ft) down. Persistence paid off and after seven years' work they recovered 99% of the bullion.

Armoured Suits

One alternative for deep diving would be to protect the diver completely from pressure in an armoured tube or suit. He would then breathe air at atmospheric pressure and therefore not suffer from 'bends' or from 'nitrogen narcosis' that comes with deep diving. The most primitive version of this idea was probably Lethbridge's tube of 1715, although the diver's hands and arms had suffered from being outside. An American, W.H. Taylor, produced a complete armoured dress in 1838. It had articulated joints, but left the hands and feet outside. it would certainly not have been capable of deep diving. A more promising design was developed by Philips in 1856. The diver was enclosed in a short, thick cylinder. The legs and arms were enclosed and the hands remained inside the metal arms which terminated in a pair of nippers. More designs followed. The main difficulty lay in the joints which had to allow the diver to use his arms and legs. The 'ball and socket' joint was introduced by the Carmagnolle brothers in their suit in 1882 but water pressure made the joints progressively harder to operate at depth.

Two Australian inventors, John Buchanon and Alexander Gordon, produced a suit in 1894 which was stiffened with wires and tried it out in Scotland. The next advance was made by Giuseppe Restucci of Naples who in 1904 had proposed a solution to the 'joint problem' which was practical if complicated. The joints were to be surrounded

Joseph Peress with the armoured apparatus he developed before World War 2 and which was to become the prototype of modern one atmosphere diving suits.

by air at a higher pressure than the surrounding water. The diver would, however, stay at atmospheric pressure. Sir Robert Davis, who records many of these devices in his book, suggested in 1912 the use of a simple cylindrical tube to allow the diver to make his observations. He could either breathe through air pipes, or from a self-regenerating oxygen system.

The German firm of Neufeldt and Kuhnke had patented a form of armoured dress in 1913 which included a special 'ball and socket' joint, where the friction was reduced by ball bearings between the two halves. It was kept watertight by a strip of rubber. They developed this further in 1920 and the joint proved successful. The diver breathed oxygen from tanks around his back and the final version was equipped with a pair of nippers. Further development of the suit followed its use by the Italian salvage company, Sorima, on the wreck of the *Egypt*. The *Egypt* had sunk in 120m (400ft) of water in 1922 with a million pounds worth of bullion on board. The recovery of the bullion was thought to be impossible with the stormy conditions and the depth, 50km (30 miles) out in the open Atlantic. Yet the Italians, after finding the wreck in 1930, successfully recovered the bullion.

Diving on the *Egypt* they used an improved, simplified Kuhnke suit with only six joints, one at each shoulder and two in each leg. They later found that a simple observation tube which they called 'the eye' which was in telephone contact with their vessel, the *Artiglio*, was most efficient. The diver directed the placing of explosive charges to blast through the deck to the strongroom and then directed the grab which raised the gold ingots.

In 1919 Joseph Peress was planning a new armoured suit in England. His second model was built in 1930 and was an improvement on the Neufeldt and Kuhnke suit in that the joints were sealed in liquid to avoid the effect of water pressure. It had weights that were removable in an emergency and claws that could be manipulated from inside. It was successfully tested in Scotland's Loch Ness by Peress's chief mechanic, Jim Jarrett who found that the joints moved freely at a depth of 136m (447ft). In 1935 the Peress suit, known as the *Tritonia*, was taken out to test on the famous wreck of the *Lusitania*, torpedoed off Kinsale Head during World War I and rumoured to contain treasure. The wreck was found by Captain Russell of the Orphir in 95m (312ft) of water and Jarrett was lowered on to the wreck on 26 October 1935.

The war interrupted the salvage activities and afterwards diving developed into other fields.

2
The Autonomous Diver and Frogman

Early Autonomous Diving Appratus

In his earliest attempts to return to the sea, man had emulated the marine animals but had been unable to hold his breath for more than a few minutes. He thus developed the systems we have described, in which air was pumped down to him in diving bells, diving helmets and armoured dresses.

Lethbridge had been an exception to the rule but he was still linked to the surface and his operations were limited in duration and depth.

In 1825 an Englishman, William H. James, designed a self-contained, compressed air diving apparatus in which the air was held in a circular iron reservoir worn around the diver's waist. The air was compressed to 30 atmospheres and James estimated that this would be enough for an hour's diving. It was a promising and workable design but unfortunately there is no record of its ever having been used.

Condert's Contribution

The credit for the first autonomous walking dress should go therefore to an American machinist, Charles Condert, employed in a factory opposite the East River in Brooklyn. In 1831 Condert had produced his apparatus, which consisted of a suit incorporating a flexible helmet which was provided with a continuous air flow from a horseshoe shaped reservoir. The suit was made of cloth coated with gum elastic and was worn with rubber shoes. A glass plate was fixed opposite the eyes. The reservoir was a copper pipe, six inches in diameter and four feet long, closed at both ends, and was worn around the waist with the two ends projecting in front of the diver on each side. Condert made a pump from a gun barrel to charge his 'reservoir'. A small valve at one end of the reservoir let air into the suit when necessary. The suit was than kept inflated and water was prevented from entering. Expired air went into the top of the hood where it was expelled through a small hole the size of a pinhead in the cloth.

Condert descended a 'shot line' and while diving held another line attached to his shot weight on the bottom. He could thus find his way back. 90kg (200lbs) of lead was loaded on to his reservoir.

The intrepid inventor went down many times in the East River to a depth of 6m (20ft). Unfortunately he suffered an accident while underwater in 1832 which resulted in the breaking of the tube which connected the reservoir to the suit, and a quick death.

Mechanic's Magazine, describing the incident in 1835 said: 'Like Mr Spalding, the improver of the diving bell, he perished in the prosecution of his favourite pursuits. The description of his dress will probably be the only memorial of this ingenious, persevering and unfortunate mechanic.'

In 1863 another American, T. Cato McKeen, took up Condert's ideas and patented an 'improved diving apparatus'. McKeen described one or more containers of compressed air, one or more air bags or buoys and a rubber suit. The container was to be mounted on the diver's back by shoulder straps and made of sheet copper in the shape of a knapsack. The really interesting point was the provision of air bags which could be filled with air from a second cylinder and inflated to bring the diver to the surface. McKeen may therefore have been the first to postulate the idea of an adjustable buoyancy lifejacket.

The First Regulator
A more practical semi-autonomous air diving apparatus was developed by a French mining engineer, Benoit Rouquayrol and Lt Auguste Denayrouze, of the French Navy in 1865. It was called the *Aerophore*. The diver carried a metal cannister on his back which contained air at a pressure of 25 to 40 atmospheres. He was normally linked to the surface and the air was kept at pressure by a pump but he could detatch the tube and be independent for a short time. Their most important development was a 'regulator' between the cannister and the breathing tube in which a membrane was subject to pressure on one side from the water and on the other from the air breathed by the diver. The air side was under lower pressure when the diver breathed in. This caused the membrane to move and open a valve to let more air in. When the diver exhaled the valve closed and the excess expired gas escaped between the lips of the 'duck's beak' valve. This was the first demand valve which automatically adjusted the pressure between the air inside and the water outside. The diver wore a nose clip but, surprisingly, Denayrouze did not recommend goggles. 'The action of sea water on the eyes is more of a tonic than otherwise,' he wrote!

In 1867 a company was formed to develop the Aerophore for

sponge diving and the equipment was despatched to the Aegean Sea. The conservative Greek sponge divers destroyed a number of sets! They were used successfully, however, at Toulon to salvage the wreck of the *Magenta*. Jules Verne in *20,000 Leagues Under the Sea* equipped Captain Nemo and his crew with an 'improved' version of the Rouquayrol-Denayrouze equipment.

Oxygen Apparatus

The first self-contained oxygen apparatus was designed by Henry Fleuss, an Englishman, in 1878. The Fleuss apparatus was built by Siebe Gorman and Co. and Sir Robert Davis later developed it as a submarine escape apparatus. Fleuss' first apparatus consisted of a mask of rubber-proofed fabric that covered the whole face, a breathing bag and a copper cylinder filled with oxygen to a pressure of 30 atmospheres. They were both attached to the diver's back together with a box of CO_2 absorbent. The diver breathed in and out of the bag and his exhaled carbon dioxide was absorbed. Occasionally he would re-purify the mixture with more oxygen and could therefore last for comparatively long periods compared with early open circuit compressed air apparatus. Alexander Lambert used it successfully in the Severn Tunnel in 1882 as already described.

The bag and cylinder were eventually moved to the front of the diver and became the type of re-breather that could ideally be used by 'frogmen' who could not afford to make tell-tale bubbles. Sir Robert Davis experimented producing a number of designs based on these models during the early years of the twentieth century.

Twentieth Century Designs

The Dragerwerk Company in Germany also developed autonomous oxygen apparatus. In 1912 they produced a first underwater sledge, designed by Captain Valentiner. This was towed over the sea bed and operated by a diver breathing from oxygen cylinders.

The pioneer of underwater films, J.E. Williamson, used independent oxygen apparatus while filming his version of Verne's *20,000 Leagues Under the Sea* in 1915.

Compressed Air

Meanwhile others were still thinking about compressed air. One of the main problems was that industry could not at this time provide cylinders that would withstand the pressure of air needed for long stays at depth. However in 1900 Louis Bouton, a pioneer of underwater photography, produced a compressed air breathing set which included a cylinder that could be charged to nearly 200 atmospheres' pressure.

One of the most successful independent compressed air devices must have been that produced by the ingenious Mr Ohgushi of Japan. *Ohgushi's Peerless Respirator* as it was known was registered as British patent no. 131,390 on 15 June 1918. The respirator could be used with one or two cylinders or with a line to the surface. Perhaps it owed something to James and Condert as the patent showed that the air could be valved from cylinders on the back to a flexible bag in the form of a belt round the diver, which compensated for the surrounding sea pressure. The diver wore a mask, remarkably similar to present day models, which covered the eyes and nose. The mask included a number of air valves and inlets. To breathe the diver clenched his teeth against a valve and breathed in through his nose. To exhale he opened his teeth and exhaled through his mouth! The difficulty of undertaking this complicated procedure under stress can be imagined. According to the Tokyo Submarine Industrial Company that manufactured it, the apparatus was adopted by the Japanese navy and was used in 1918–19 on the wreck of the Norwegian steamer *Calendar* and the British ship *Nile*, both at a depth of 60m (200ft). It was apparently used even deeper to collect coral and the traditional Japanese diver certainly seemed to have a remarkable resistance to nitrogen narcosis and decompression sickness. In spite of all this the device appears to have remained largely unknown outside Japan

The First Mass-Produced Equipment.
All diving equipment up to this time had naturally been designed for use either by the inventor himself or by professionals. The first man to envisage a large number of amateur divers taking to the sea was a flier who dreamt also of flying in the sea. His name was Yves Le Prieur. He began diving in 1905 with the French Navy.

In 1925 he watched a demonstration of an underwater blow-lamp used to cut metal. The diver used breathing equipment produced by another Frenchman, Maurice Fernez, around 1912. This was extremely lightweight and consisted of a small V-shaped metal tube, fitted with a mouth piece connected by a simple rubber tube to the traditional pump on the surface. The right hand end of the metal tube ended in a rubber flap or 'duck beak' valve that allowed air to escape but no water to enter. A nose clip, a detachable weight belt and a pair of Fernez goggles completed the outfit. Le Prieur envisaged the use of the equipment for sport divers but the first thing that would have to go would be the tube to the surface.

He visited the inventor and in 1926 they together produced the 'Prieur-Fernez' apparatus. The main difference was that the diver now had a cylinder of compressed air attached to his back. Le Prieur continued to improve the apparatus. In 1933 the new 'Le Prieur Diving Apparatus' appeared. The painful goggles and disagreeable nose clip were replaced by a mask which covered the whole face. The air was supplied at low pressure from the cylinder, now again positioned in front of the diver, and escaped in bubbles around the mask. In 1934 Le Prieur gave a series of demonstrations to the public, chiefly in the Trocadero in Paris and in 1935 he and Jean Painlevé founded the first amateur diving club using the new apparatus. This was known as the *'Club des Scaphandres et de la Vie Sous L'Eau'*.

Le Prieur's apparatus was still not perfect. The air was largely wasted and the air pressure had to be manually ajusted during the course of the dive. Le Prieur, a prolific inventor, turned out the first underwater gun, powered by compressed air, and a very effective model, *'The Nautilus'*, which actually fired a charge of black powder in a blank cartridge sending a heavy harpoon twenty yards through the water. He also made a foam rubber protective diving suit that he filled with hot water.

So many new devices were produced by the new race of amateur breath-hold divers in the 1930s that it is difficult to document them in strictly chronological order.

Development of the Mask and Snorkel

A small family of underwater spearfishermen had been operating on the Mediterranean coast of France since the 1920s. They used goggles and spears only on breath-hold dives, descending feet first and swimming breast-stroke in search of sea bream and groupers. The first of these pioneers was an American, Guy Gilpatric, an ex-flier and writer who first hunted using an old pair of his flying goggles plugged up with putty and painted over. In 1928 he wrote an entertaining book on the new sport, *The Compleat Goggler*, now much sought after by collectors. Gilpatric inspired those who watched his technique and these included Jacques Cousteau, Philippe Tailliez and Hans Hass, who were later to surpass him in technique and experience.

Gilpatric never used flippers or fins, but the prototypes had appeared in 1929 and they had been patented in 1933. The inventor was a Frenchman, Commandant de Corlieu, who put them on the market in 1935. Some years later another American, Owen Churchill, discovered them and produced them under licence from de Corlieu in the States. They were then re-imported across the Atlantic for the use of Allied frogmen during World War 2.

Although Fernez had produced effective goggles that were eventually used by Gilpatric and his friends, the production of an efficient diving mask probably dates from 1932 when Alec Kramarenko, an expatriot Russian who had lived in Japan and seen pearl divers there, produced his first pair in a wooden frame. He discovered that the two eye-pieces of conventional goggles gave double vision and so he produced a single pane for both eyes. He tried replacing the wooden mask with metal, dental cement and celluloid. Finally he made a mould and poured in molten rubber. In September 1937 he took out a patent and began to sell his masks. Experience showed that below 6m (20ft) or so water pressure squeezed the single pane mask painfully due to the increasing pressure. Kramarenko copied a Japanese model and fixed a soft rubber bulb at each side of the mask. The increasing pressure squeezed these, effectively forcing more air into the mask. Enthusiasts as far away as California also produced single pane goggles of this type.

The final solution was found by a Frenchman, Maxime Forjot, who patented a mask which covered not only eyes but also the nose. All the diver then had to do was to blow a little air into his mask through his nose to prevent the pressure effect.

The diver still had to turn his head to the side to breathe on the surface. Gilpatric had tried a flexible metal covered breathing tube without success. He mentions, however, that Steve Butler, a local Englishman had produced a successful snorkel tube with which he swam on the surface for hours without lifting his head. Commandant Tailliez was among those experimenting and made his first snorkel tube from a piece of his heavy garden hose. The first patent came out in 1938 under the name of Forjot. The diver could then spend hours looking down at the sea bed and preparing for his short breath-hold dives.

Gilpatric and the original 'gogglers' transfixed fish with simple spears. The first harpoon gun powered by a spring was patented by Kramarenko in 1937 and another type by Forjot in 1938. A different school of thought was led by Georges Beuchat in Marseilles and used harpoon guns with powerful rubber bands which catapulted a metal arrow.

Commeinhes and the Aqualung
But what of the 'serious sinkers' that Gilpatric had envisaged in his

book? The almost unknown Georges Commeinhes was the first heir to Le Prieur. He was a young spear fisherman and his father ran a well-known business manufacturing valves for mining equipment. Georges adapted the family apparatus for diving. Commandant Tailliez relates that Commeinhes was considered very amateur and 'completely mad' by his father and family. However Georges Commeinhes had produced the first fully automatic aqualung. The cylinder was worn on the back with a full face mask. Air escaped from a special valve opposite the air intake instead of around the mask as in the Le Prieur apparatus. The demand valve was mounted between the shoulder blades and it was supplied with a pressure gauge to give an indication of how much air was left. The cylinder was filled with compressed air to 150 atmospheres' pressure.

The first Commeinhes aqualung was approved by the French War Office in June 1937. Later Commeinhes swam down on a demonstration dive to a depth of 52m (170ft). His model GC-47 was manufactured and had great potential. Unfortunately Georges Commeinhes was killed in the battle for the liberation of Strasbourg during World War 2.

Hans Hass

Hans Hass, a young school leaver from Vienna, had come across Gilpatric on the Riviera in 1937. In Hass' own words he 'met his destiny' that day, being fascinated by Gilpatric's underwater hunting. Hass decided to take photographs and films rather than just to fish. In 1938 he led his first expedition to Dalmatia. It was a light-hearted affair but Hass took his first successful underwater photographs. The students used their own primitive home-made helmets and their own lungs. Hass planned his next expedition to the Red Sea while the war clouds were gathering over Europe but finally decided on the Island of Curacao in the Dutch West Indies. He and his friends took the first close-ups of sharks while breath-hold diving. They were still underwater fishing when the world war broke out in September 1939.

Jacques Cousteau

Another Frenchman had also been searching to develop an easy, efficient aqualung. He was Jacques Cousteau, a French Navy officer. He was put on shore duty at Toulon while recovering from a bad car accident. There his fellow officer, Philippe Taillez, gave him his first pair of goggles. They soon became expert hunters emulating their idol, Gilpatric. Tailliez met Frederic Dumas, the best underwater fisherman along the Var, on the beach and a friendship sprang up between Tailliez, Dumas and Cousteau that was to lead to the creation of a new sport.

Cousteau's first trials with the Le Prieur apparatus convinced him of the potential of the new exploration sport and also of the imperfection of that equipment. In 1938 he made his first breathing set – a very amateur version of the Davis escape apparatus using oxygen. He suffered from oxygen convulsions. He persisted in 1939 but was finally convinced of the dangers of oxygen for sport diving. The outbreak of war in 1939 split the team but they got together again in 1940 after the fall of France. Cousteau quietly made his first film, *Ten Fathoms Under the Sea*.

In November 1942 Tailliez and Cousteau were given leave and Cousteau left Toulon for Paris to try to get permission to make underwater documentary films. There he met an engineer, Emile Gagnan, who had been working on a device to run cars on coal gas supplied through pressure valves. Gagnan produced a version of his 'demand regulator' for Cousteau and they linked it to a cylinder of compressed air and tried it out on the River Marne. Their valve worked but was still not perfect. When Cousteau swam upright the air poured into his mouth but when he swam head-downwards he had to struggle to get enough. They discussed the problem and agreed that the exhaust valve should be at the same level and in the same 'box'. The air would come 'on demand' and the valve would be situated as close as possible to the level of the diver's lungs in the middle of his back. There would be two breathing tubes, one for inhalation and one for exhalation. Tailliez arrived for the first trial of the new aqualung when it arrived at Bandol in June 1943. Cousteau tried it out first, gliding down to a depth of 18m (60ft). 'Now at last we have time to explore the silent world,' he wrote.

Although the 'three musketeers' – Cousteau, Tailliez and Dumas – now had the means, the war that was raging around them did not give them the time.

World War 2, The Frogmen
The military applications of free diving had first been realised and exploited by the Italians. On 19 September 1941 a Royal Navy tanker, the *Denbydale* that had been lying securely in harbour in Gibraltar, suddenly shook as five hundred pounds of explosive went off shattering her plates and turning her into a useless hulk.

This was the result of five years work started off by two young Italian naval architects, Tesei and Toschi. Their first blueprint for a human torpedo was produced in 1935 and soon the Italians had formed their own special 'H Group' to operate it. Their first operations against the British in the Mediterranean were abortive. Toschi was captured but the British had no idea what his mission was or of the new form of warfare. The human torpedo was 6.7m (22ft) long with a 0.53m (21in) diameter. Its detachable warhead held 227 kilos (500lb) of high explosive. It was driven by batteries operating two propellers. Two divers sat astride it wearing oxygen sets and managed to keep their seats at its maximum speed of three knots. The crew approached their targets with their chins above the water and then dived under the enemy ship. They clamped a line from the warhead to the keel and detached it. They could then return using the remainder of the craft.

The Attacks in Gibraltar Harbour

Further unsuccessful attacks followed and Tesei and a number of others were captured. The British became aware of the potential dangers of this new midget craft. Two Royal Navy Lieutenants, 'Bill' Bailey and 'Buster' Crabb were formed into the nucleus of an attack party to try to stop the Italians and remove their charges. Bailey was already acting as Diving Officer when Crabb had arrived in Gibraltar as a Bomb and Mine Disposal Officer. He took him down a ladder in the harbour to introduce him to the Davis escape apparatus. The time was November 1942. Crabb was thirty-two years old, opposed to any form of physical exercise and capable of swimming only three lengths of the swimming pool. But he learnt fast. They had no underwater suits and dived in swimming trunks.

The first successful operation on the *Denbydale* had been launched from the Italian submarine *Sciré* commanded by Prince Valerio Borghese. The successful chariot commander was Lt Visintini and he escaped under submarine nets to a triumphant reception on the nearby coast of 'neutral' Spain and later in Italy.

In summer 1942 the Italians tried their individual swimmer technique in Gibraltar harbour. One charge went off prematurely and Bailey and Seaman Bell dived and discovered a new kind of midget mine pressed against the bottom of the ships by air filled balloons. Although the charge was only 2.3 kilos (5lb) it was enough to blow a 1.2m (4ft) hole in the ship's bottom. Bailey and his assistant slashed the balloons and the mines exploded harmlessly on the bottom in due course.

During the summer, Bailey was swimming on his usual checking duties when he saw an enemy figure approaching – an enemy frogman! He drew his knife and the first underwater combat of modern times began. Bailey got his knife into the Italian's rubber suit but the Italian, with his flippers, could swim faster. It is not known whether the Italian ever got back to base.

Bailey moved on shortly after this and his command was taken over by Crabb. One night in December the alarm was given after two wet and cold Italians had been found on the South Mole of Grand Harbour. A number of warships were at Gibraltar at the time and Crabb and Bell were ordered to night dive and search the bottoms of them all. The attack had involved three human torpedoes but the British depth charge defence was now more efficient and the Italians lost three of the six men involved and two of the torpedoes. No charges were placed. The Italians said that they had been launched from a parent submarine but this was only a cover story for one of the most ingenious operations in the new underwater war.

When Italy had entered the war, the 4900 tonne tanker *Olterra* was lying in Algeciras harbour and was scuttled by the crew. A disinterested 'neutral' crew from Spain was then appointed. In the summer of 1942 Visintini had the brilliant idea of turning it into a secret underwater base for the two-man torpedo attacks on Gibraltar. Whilst the Spaniards were told that the ship was being repaired Italian engineers cut a section 7.6m (25ft) long in the steel bulkhead, hinging it so that it hung like a flap. Water was pumped out of the forward tanks until the bows rose out of the water. A 1.2m (4ft) hole was cut in the side of the ship that opened into the bow compartment about 2m (6ft) below the waterline. When the ship sank back the hold was dry and the bow compartment flooded. The two-man torpedoes were then assembled in the hold and lowered into the bow to pass out through the flap 2m (6ft) below the surface.

A second operation from the *Olterra* in May 1943 was completely successful and three large ships were seriously damaged or sunk.

In September 1943 when the Italians surrendered the Governor of Algeciras heard of the *Olterra* plot and tried to destroy the evidence before the British arrived but when Crabb went aboard he found parts of three human torpedoes in good condition and reconstructed a complete torpedo from the pieces.

The peak of Italian success came with the crippling of the British battleships *Queen Elizabeth* and *Valiant* in Alexandria Harbour. Six men in three tiny craft crippled two of the most powerful ships in the world.

British Chariots
In 1942 the Admiralty had ordered the development of British human

British and Italian 'charioteers' sat astride their vehicles on the surface and underwater. They fixed detachable explosive charges to the hulls of enemy ships using hand magnets.

torpedoes. However they had to be superior in view of the fact that it was intended to use them not in the clear comparatively warm waters of the Mediterranean, but in the cold fjords of Norway.

Already frogmen had suffered from the effects of oxygen poisoning and the first test of a closed circuit oxygen-nitrogen mixture was started by autumn 1942. With this mixture the frogmen doubled their depth capability. The need now was to recover and immobilise mines such as the new German magnetic mine. A special mine recovery suit was developed and this was used with three aluminium cylinders strapped to the diver's back.

In 1943 the first British mobile, amphibious 'dry' suit was perfected. It was known as the 'Sladen Suit' or more coloquially 'Clammy Death'! It included a built-in breathing bag, connected to a full face mask and oxygen bottles salvaged from German aircraft. A canister

Royal Navy divers showing the dress and equipment used in World War 2. The figure on the left is a port clearance diver, while that on the right is a human torpedo 'charioteer'.

of soda-lime absorbed the carbon dioxide exhaled into the bag.

After a successful raid with canoes on the French coast the Royal Marines commissioned a new design. This proved to be a tiny free flooding canoe that could travel underwater as well as on the surface and was the smallest and least detectable craft ever made. The canoe carried one diver in a reclining position and so became known as the Sleeping Beauty. She was developed by a young officer, Quentin Reeves, who claimed to be able to loop the loop underwater in her.

The operators of the new British two-man chariots sat on saddles in Sladen suits. The leading crew member operated the controls which were simple. A rudder was operated by a joy stick which was moved from side to side to turn, and forwards and back to sink and rise. There was a combined starter and throttle and the electic motor had three forward speeds and one reverse. Top speed was three and a half knots. Finally, there were two pump levers to pump water in or out of the tank in the bow or stern and a lever to open or shut the ballast tank amidships. 'Number 2' was responsible for operating the cutters and for attaching the explosive head on arrival. All worked very well in theory but practice could be very different. The crew practised manoeuvering the craft, leaving it and moving over ships' bottoms using hand magnets to attach the detachable warheads. Finally they learned to do it all in darkness! There were a number of operations using chariots. In summer 1942 it was decided to use them to attack the German battleship *Tirpitz*. Churchill, leading the British war effort, was very concerned with the activities of this huge 56,000 tonne German battleship which was tying up the British home fleet from her anchorage in the north of Norway as she menaced the British convoys to Russia. A daring operation was launched in summer 1942 from a small fishing boat, the *Arthur*, skippered by a Norwegian Leif Larsen DSM CGM, which set out from Shetland with two chariots lashed to her deck. During the rough crossing to Norway the chariots were transferred to the sea and towed out of sight, just astern of the *Arthur*. When she entered Trondheim Fjord, a German control officer boarded her, looked at her papers and authorised her continuing. The six British frogmen were hidden in the hold. Unfortunately, after having got so far, a sudden wave caused the wires towing the subs to slacken and then become taut. They broke and both were lost. All the crew escaped successfully into Sweden.

The next operation was at Tripoli in Libya, where chariots helped to immobilise block ships in the harbour entrance and to survey the Sicilian coast prior to the Allied invasion. At Palermo a single chariot sank a cruiser and severely damaged a cargo ship.

The cheekiest attack of all was in the harbour of the main Italian Naval Base at La Spezia in February 1944. A British chariot was dropped by a motor boat seven miles from the harbour. The crew travelled on the surface until they were in the harbour entrance, then, alternately diving to avoid detection and surfacing to check their positions they managed to cut their way through six anti-submarine nets which delayed them until almost daybreak. They closed on to their target, the 10,000 tonne cruiser *Bolzano*, placed four magnets on her bottom and sank the warhead of the torpedo lashed to them. The fuse was set for two hours. They managed to get ashore, although the batteries of the torpedo were exhausted. At six thirty a.m. the *Bolzano* exploded, rolled over and sank in a quarter of an hour.

The Gamma Group

Meantime the inventive Italians had formed a 'gamma' group of swimmers to harass the Allies from neutral harbours. One brilliant operation was carried out single handed by Sub-Lieutenant Luigi Ferraro.

The Turkish port of Alexandretta was used by the Allies to load chromium for the war effort and steamers were anchored just over a mile from the coast to pick it up. Ferraro had been a physical education student in Tripoli and combined the qualities of determination and physical courage. He was disguised as a consular employee and joined the Italian Vice-Consulate in Alexandretta. Even the Italian diplomats knew nothing of his secret mission. It was a difficult area in which to work, a small frontier town full of intrigue with six consulates, American, British, French, Greek, German and Italian all close together and facing the sea. Ferraro had one accomplice, a consulate clerk, Giovanni Roccardi, who was really a Lieutenant in the Italian Navy Secret Service. Ferraro was introduced into the local fashionable society and he excelled in drinking and dancing and geniality. In the mornings he was on the beach although it soon became clear that he was a non-swimmer! In the early evenings he and Roccardi played handball and bowls on the sand. On 30 June 1943 they lingered over a team game of bowls. As darkness fell Ferraro darted into the beach cabin they used and emerged clad in black rubber, fins and mask and with two strange oblong objects dangling from his waist. He disappeared soundlessly into the sea and swam 2400 metres ($1\frac{1}{2}$ miles) to the 7000 tonne Greek steamer *Orion*. Under the beam of the searchlights on board he slipped along the side of the vessel, switched to oxygen breathing gear and groped down to the bilge keel to detach his charges. By 4 a.m. he was back in the consulate. A week later Orion finished loading and left. She made only a few miles before exploding and sinking. The survivors thought they had been torpedoed!

Ferraro continued to operate from Alexandretta and also the major port of Mersana. In a single month he sank two ships and severely damaged a third. After the war Luigi Ferraro, now a professor, continued his interest in diving and particularly spear fishing. He

Luigi Ferraro carried out single-handed sabotage against Allied shipping during World War 2, causing considerable damage in the ports of Alexandretta and Mersana.

became President of the World Underwater Federation (CMAS) Sports Committee and of one of the largest Italian diving equipment companies.

Development of the 'X' Craft.
Churchill's concern at the activities of the German battleship *Tirpitz* have already been referred to and, following the failure of the chariots alternatives were sought. Commander John Varley had been working on the design of a midget submarine that could lay charges under the battleship and escape. The 'X' craft, as they became known, had a crew of four, one of whom was a diver. The diver operated out of a 'diver lock-out', then known as 'wet and dry', compartment which could be flooded.

The *Tirpitz* was protected by her own guns, instant smoke screens, a mine field, listening posts, patrols, anti-submarine booms and finally nets. She lay deep in Altenfjord in Northern Norway.

The 'X' craft proved to be small enough to cross the mine fields which started only 4.5m (15ft) below the surface, strong enough to submerge to 90m (300ft), powerful enough to destroy the strongest battleship in the world and versatile enough to avoid detection, cut through nets, have a 36 hour endurance and a 500km (300 mile) range. The prototype was launched in the Hamble River in March 1942 and at the beginning of 1943 the first operational models arrived from Vickers. They were 14.6m (48ft) long, weighing 39 tonnes. As the inside deck height was only 1.4m ($4\frac{1}{2}$ft) the unfortunate crew had to crouch, sit, squat or crawl to operate them. They were run by batteries underwater and by a 40 horse-power London bus engine on the surface! Along the sides were fixed detachable charges, each containing two tonnes of Amatex explosive with a clockwork time fuse.

The call went out for volunteers for 'special and hazardous duty' and the first crews were formed. Six 'X' craft set out for the *Tirpitz* but only three arrived to attack her. Their Commanders were a quiet pipe-smoking Scot, Donald Cameron (X-6), a dapper unassuming Englishman, Godfrey Place (X-7) and a red haired Australian, 'Tiger' Henty-Creer (X-5). The tiny midget subs were towed across the North Sea by parent conventional submarines, while manned by 'passage' crews. On the evening of 20 September 1943 they were cast off and began the long perilous voyage through the mine fields off the coast and down the 80km (50 miles) of fjords to the *Tirpitz* anchorage in Kaafjord. The new X-craft suffered from misty periscopes, unreliable compasses and had to surface to check their position frequently.

Cameron was seen as he approached *Tirpitz* and was fired on. Escape seemed impossible and X-6 dived for the last time, scraping along the hull of the battleship to release her charges set to explode in one hour. Cameron and his crew were picked up by the Germans after they had scuttled X-6.

Godfrey Place successfully released his charges under the giant battleship and tried to escape over the top of the anti-submarine net. Increasingly accurate fire from the *Tirpitz* brought his X-craft to a standstill. He clambered out into the hail of bullets and managed to swim to a target vessel nearby. The vents had been opened and the X-7 suddenly sank before the rest of the crew could get out. On the bottom at 37m (120ft) Bob Aitken, the diver, explained to the others how the Davis escape apparatus worked. All three donned their sets as the icy water rose round their ankles and knees. Suddenly a fuse blew and they were in pitch darkness, and surrounded by fumes and smoke. This meant breathing through the sets early. They tried to conserve oxygen and waited for the submarine to flood completely so that they could open the hatch. With oxygen nearly finished Aitken felt about for the others. Their bags were flat and they had stopped breathing! He struggled to open the hatch and passed out. He next remembered coming up in a shower of bubbles and being picked up by the Germans to be taken onto the *Tirpitz*.

The Britons set their watches and said nothing. Right on time the charges exploded and the huge battleship rose five feet out of the water. Steam gushed out covering the water and injured and dead were brought from below. The battleship heeled, still afloat, but crippled.

Soon after X-5 surfaced off the starboard bow and the *Tirpitz* opened fire. The submarine disappeared in an eddy of foam.

Donald Cameron and Godfrey Place returned from German prisoner-of-war camps after the war to receive Victoria Crosses. Place stayed in the Royal Navy and rose to the rank of Admiral. There was no trace of X-5 or Tiger Henty-Creer. She was claimed as sunk but there had been reports of sightings of a periscope returning northwards after the attack. Many years later a party of British Sub-Aqua Club divers searched the fjord for her but without success (see chapter 3). The mystery of what happened to X-5 still remains.

Underwater Demolition
As 'D' day, planned for the Allied invasion of Europe, approached, there was an enormous demand for divers and new equipment. They would be clearing the beaches and harbours for landing craft and the new amphibious tanks. Captain Bill Shelford RN organised the production of equipment and training for several hundred new divers.

The special parties that cleared ports had to work deeper than 9m (30ft) and so used the oxy-nitrogen mixtures. The approaches to the main invasion beaches were marked by two X-craft flashing their lights. The first men ashore on 3 June 1944 were 120 frogmen of the 'landing craft obstruction clearance units'. The Germans had a series of formidable obstacles including two and a half tonne masses of steel constructed like picket fences. The four Royal Navy and six Royal Marine units worked in the face of shell, mortar and sniper fire. They wore newly developed neoprene suits with helmets, breathing apparatus and fins, for the first time. The swimming fins had been ordered by Lieutenant Bruce Wright of the Canadian Navy who had used them in California before the war. A splendid addition was a blast proof 'kapok' jacket worn underneath. This successfully saved the lives of many men when shells and mortars exploded in the water close to them. On 'D' day these divers blasted a gap 1000m ($\frac{5}{8}$ mile) wide in the defences covering the invasion beach. Commandos then poured through with guns blazing.

The ports presented a different problem. Here the Germans had

A British frogman wearing the suit that was developed in World War 2 for use in attacks on enemy harbours, installations and shipping.

planted non-magnetic and acoustic mines with clockwork fuses set to go off in periods of up to 80 days. For this work 'P' parties of human mine sweepers were trained. They searched harbours such as Cherbourg for the new mines. At first they used lifelines but then they developed buoyant rubber floats to indicate the diver's position. This idea was borrowed from the navy many years later by amateur divers and is now standard practice in British waters.

Lieutenant 'Bill' Bailey of Gibraltar fame commanded another group that successfully cleared the inland port of Caen and its lock gates that had been booby-trapped.

The 'P' parties went on to clear Boulogne, Calais, Dieppe, Ostend, Le Havre and Antwerp. At Antwerp 32km (20 miles) of walls had to be cleared in the ice, snow and fog of winter. The divers often worked up to their necks in mud and a number were killed by German long range rockets. These 'clearance' divers were not at first recognised by the RN Diving Schools but eventually became the most important and experienced divers in the Royal Navy.

Germany did not use frogmen or underwater saboteurs until quite late in the war. However in 1944 a team of their finest Navy swimmers were in training near Venice, experimenting with underwater equipment copied from the Italians.

In October the British forces were supplying their advance over two bridges at Nijmegen. It was essential to the Germans that these bridges be destroyed but it was impractical to bomb them due to the strength of the RAF and the ground defences. The Waal River had a strong current which ran from German-held territory through the British lines and out again into German-held areas. A plan evolved to float cylindrical high-explosive charges of neutral bouyancy down the river. The German frogmen would then attach them to the bridges and later they would be exploded with a delayed action fuse.

Six charges were prepared, two for the railway bridge and four for the road bridge. The plan was that the swim would take place at night. Four frogmen would be detailed to take the two railway bridge charges which would be roped together and would be towed down the river 6m (20ft) apart. Eight frogmen would control the remaining four charges which were also roped together in a square pattern. When the charge arrived each leading pair would have to straddle a pier of the bridge with their bowline to stop further movement and then the charges would be sunk to the bottom. The frogmen would dive using oxygen to operate the fuse mechanism. Then both parties would continue downriver until coloured rockets were fired to show them the friendly zone.

They managed to set their charges and continued downstream for 10.5km (6½ miles) until they saw a coloured rocket fired from well inside the German held area, away from the river so as not to arouse suspicion. They came ashore believing all their problems were over only to be captured by a patrol of Dutch underground forces on reconnaisance ahead of the British lines. Two Germans were killed as they tried to escape.

The railway bridge charge blew wrecking one of the spans. Only two of the charges under the road bridge exploded. Damage was caused but the bridges were not destroyed.

Far-Eastern Activity

As the war in Europe drew to a close with the successful Allied landings, more activity took place in the Far East where Japan continued her lone battle. In European waters one of the main problems had been cold but in the Far East a water temperature of 88°F resulted in the protosorb canister of the oxygen set warming up until the warm oxygen gave sore mouths to the swimmers and the temperature inside the suits reached over 100°F sapping vitality. Special lightweight gear was gradually developed and the X-craft were redesigned to include an air-conditioning unit (XE models).

One of the first successful operations was the cutting of the Saigon-Singapore and Saigon-Hong Kong undersea cables. Lieutenant Shean, DSO RANVR, who had operated in Norway took the modified X-craft, XE-4, equipped with a special grapnel into position off Singapore and located the cables. They were successfully cut by the X-craft's diver.

One of the most outstanding attacks took place on 30 July 1945. XE-3 commanded by Lieutenant Ian Fraser was towed by a parent submarine until she was near Singapore and released at 11.00 p.m. He navigated her through a mine field that night and by morning they fixed their position at 13Km (8 miles) off Johore. By 5.00 a.m. they had made their way well into the Johore Strait. The crew cat-napped and took Benzedrine tablets to ward off sleep. By 8 a.m. the X-craft was 5.5km ($3\frac{1}{2}$ miles) off the boom and increased speed. She passed through the boom gate without incident. At 12.05 a.m. they sighted their target, the Japanese heavy cruiser *Takao*. At 2.00 p.m. Fraser put XE-3 down to 6.7m (22ft) and she bumped along the bottom of the Johore Strait until she crashed against a solid object which they presumed to be the *Takao*. The depth was only 4.6m (15ft) and it was felt too dangerous to let the diver, Leading Seaman Magennis, leave the submarine to fix the limpet mines with which the XE-craft were fitted as he would be seen through the clear water. They tried to move but were stuck! After 10 minutes of manoeuvring the XE staggered out of the hole into which she had fallen and reached daylight.

It was getting late and Fraser decided on a final plan. He 'bottom-crawled' under the ship until they 'fell' into a 7.3m (24ft) patch under the middle of the *Takao*. The depth was 6.7m (22ft).

Magennis checked his oxygen apparatus and left the submarine. He fixed six limpets on the bottom of the *Takao* after scraping off several years' growth of seaweed and barnacles. Magennis found that the water was murky. After he returned Fraser jettisoned his side charges and high explosives only to find that the starboard charge carrier had stuck. Magennis left the XE-3 again with a large spanner and in spite of exhaustion levered the release pins and dropped the charge. He came back to the 'wet and dry' compartment at 4.39 p.m. Fraser's problems were not yet over, however. Large amounts of fresh water were affecting the trim of the submarine and she actually broke surface for 6 seconds a mile from the *Takao*. She finally escaped to the boom and her crew were picked up by the parent submarine at 3 a.m.

The charges blew a huge hole in the hull of the *Takao* and immobilized her for a considerable time.

Both Fraser and Magennis were awarded the Victoria Cross.

After the war Ian Fraser set up a diving company with his brother. They also obtained a large portable tank and produced a travelling entertainment illustrating frogmen activities. The firm became North Sea Diving Services and Ian Fraser is still active in the North Sea diving industry.

The Mystery of Crabb
Two British frogmen, Buster Crabb of Gibraltar and Jimmy Hodges who had been in X-craft in Normandy, continued in the Navy after the war. In January 1950, when the submarine *Truculent* sank to the bottom where the current was too strong for helmet divers they swam down and entered her hatch to check for survivors. Hodges later took the first pictures of torpedoes leaving submarines. Later be joined Hans Hass on an expedition to the West Indies but died of oxygen poisoning on a deep reef there.

The fate of Buster Crabb was mysterious and bizarre. By 1955 he had been retired from the Navy but still hankered after the life he had enjoyed. In the middle of April 1956 the Russian cruiser *Ordzhonikidze* with two attendant destroyers docked at Portsmouth bringing the Russian leaders, Bulganin and Kruschev, to Britain. Crabb arrived in Portsmouth on 17 April and booked into the Sallyport Hotel with a Mr. Smith. On 19 April Crabb disappeared. 'Mr. Smith' collected his belongings and a Royal Navy Captain announced that Crabb had disappeared on underwater tests. The press became really interested when it was discovered that the Portsmouth police had removed four pages from the Sallyport Hotel register, mentioning the official Secrets Act. Questions were tabled in the House of Commons. Colleagues wondered if he had been working for a British military intelligence group. If he had been examining the Russian cruiser he would have been diving deeper than the safe limit of 10m (33ft) and so oxygen poisoning was a distinct possibility. The Prime Minister told the House that 'it would not be in the public interest to discuss the circumstances'. Moscow Radio broadcast the text of the notes exchanged by the two governments. The Russians had complained that frogmen had been observed floating between the Soviet destroyers at 7.30 a.m. on the morning of 19 April and complained of espionage. The British Government and Foreign Office denied all knowledge.

During the following years there were unconfirmed reports that Crabb had been seen in the USSR training teams of frogmen. It seems more likely that he met his death in the grey depths of Portsmouth harbour during the early hours of that April morning.

Post-War Resumption of Activity

As soon as the War was over in 1945 the pioneers of underwater exploration, Hans Hass and Jacques Cousteau, set out to explore and document the underwater world.

Hass organised his long-delayed expedition to the Red Sea in 1949 and produced an excellent film and book, entitled *Under the Red Sea*, on his return.The first of his evocative books to be published in Britain, *Diving to Adventure*, had appeared a few months before Cousteau's *The Silent World* in 1953. His yacht *Xarifa* and his underwater adventures together with his wife Lotte, provided the first exciting underwater series on television.

Cousteau's book, *The Silent World*, had charted the adventures of the new pioneers of the aqualung and his film of the same name became a classic. In 1950 Cousteau also acquired a ship, an ex-British minesweeper bought with the aid of the Guinness family. He renamed it *Calypso* and it provided a base for a series of expeditions and took his team to many parts of the world's oceans. His television films helped to finance further cruises and new and more sophisticated equipment to explore the 'silent world'.

The formation of the 'Cousteau Society' in 1974 provided him with a non-profit making organisation devoted to preserving the sea for future generations. Following the tragic death of his son Philippe who was also the Society's chief film artist in the crash of their flying boat, *Flying Calypso*, in 1979 Cousteau spent his time partly at sea, partly in the USA and Paris and partly at Monaco where he is director of the Oceanographic Museum.

3
Growth of a New Sport

The creation of an effective and simple means of swimming beneath the surface had been a gradual process. However there is no doubt that the successful marketing of the aqualung or SCUBA (Self Contained Underwater Breathing Apparatus), as it became known in the United States, was due to the drive of Jacques Cousteau. His book converted thousands to the new sport of underwater swimming and his films, together with those of Hans Hass, produced an army of enthusiasts of all ages anxious to take up the new sport.

The production and marketing of the perfected apparatus in France provided the means for amateur divers to explore the shallow seas around the coasts of the world and created the fastest growing sport of the 1960s and 1970s. The potentially dangerous nature of the sport led to the production of handbooks and manuals and also to the formation of aqualung diving clubs in which beginners could share their training and experience.

Around the World
France

The earliest diving clubs were probably those set up in France using Le Prieur's apparatus, but the first aqualung club was the *Club Alpin Sous-Marin* which was formed in Cannes by Henri Broussard in 1946 when the aqualung first became available there. The club was really more of a school supplying the necessary equipment and tuition. In 1947 Louis Lehoux started the *Club de la Mer* and Marcel Isy-Schwartz the *Club des Chasseurs Sous-Marin de France*. By 1948 there were already eight true clubs in existence in France with over 700 members.

Borelli, one of the early French aqualungers foresaw the rapid growth of the sport and suggested the formation of a federation of diving clubs. As a result the *Fédération des Sociétes de Pêche à la Nage et d'Etudes Sous-Marines* was formed in 1948. At about the same time Dr Clerc was also forming a federation. As the objects were very similar the two organisations amalagamated to become the *Fédération Francais d'Etudes et de Sports Sous-Marins* in 1955 with Borelli as president and Clerc as vice-president. The new federation grew to become the recognised body for amateur diving in France. Jacques Dumas, an international lawyer and one of the original French federation committee members, guided its growth and influence and later became general secretary of the World Underwater Federation (*Confederation Mondiale des Activités Sub-Aquatiques*) when it was formed in 1959. The number of clubs affiliated to it increased until, by the mid 1970s, there were no less than 700.

Italy-Spain-Benelux

Early aqualungs were bought in France by visiting sportsmen who often returned to form clubs in their own countries. The first Italian club was started by Gonzatti and Dr Stuart-Tovini in 1948. Many Italians had already been spearfishing and experimenting with the equipment that had been so successfully used by their frogmen during the war.

The Spaniards too had long been interested in spearfishing, the first championship having been held as early as 1942. The first spearfishing club had been started in Barcelona in 1946. Some of these Spanish underwater fishermen also experimented with Italian frogmen's equipment after the war and in 1951 Santiago Ferran brought the first French aqualung into the country. In the same year Clemente Vidal founded the famous CRIS diving club in Barcelona and Spanish divers such as Roberto Diaz and Eduardo Admetlla chased new depth records with the aqualung.

Diving conditions in Belgium and the Netherlands were not good with only the murky, tidal English Channel, but sports diving was successfully introduced there in 1950, mainly by those with previous experience in the Mediterranean. Most diving in the Low Countries has necessarily taken place in flooded quarries and other inland open water areas because of sea conditions. Regular diving holidays are organised to the Mediterranean. The Belgian federation was formed in 1957 and in the same year Dutch clubs came together to standardize safety standards and training.

Britain

A British sports enthusiast, Colin McLeod, had discovered the fascination of using face mask, fins and snorkel tube while resting from RAF war-time flying operations in the South of France. Returning to civilian life after the war he became a director of Lillywhites, the London sports store, and in 1947 imported the first ex-frogman fins into England. The aqualung became available in Britain in 1950 and a number of clubs and schools sprang up, notably the British Underwater Centre run by another ex-RAF officer, Trevor Hampton. By 1953 there were two principal clubs, the Underwater Explorers Club and the British Sub-Aqua Club. The latter had been formed on 15 October 1953 by Oscar Gugen, a far-sighted businessman, and Peter Small, an enthusiastic journalist, together with a small band of interested amateurs. The Underwater Explorers Club collapsed soon afterwards due to financial problems but the BSAC went on growing.

The first issue of the club's magazine, *Neptune*, came out in 1954 and described the newly-elected 'General Committee's' efforts to obtain recognition, air for aqualungs and swimming pool time for training. It also describes the three commercial diving centres that were teaching the 'new art of the aqualung.' These were run by Trevor Hampton at Warfleet Creek near Dartmouth, by Bram Martin at Laughing Waters near Cobham in Kent and, further afield, by Major Simon Codrington at his Underwater Explorers Club in Libya which catered mainly for club members on holiday. The British Sub-Aqua Club also ran its own holiday programme in the South of France which was supervised by the club's first training officer, Jack Atkinson.

Soon after the formation of the BSAC in London under the chairmanship of Oscar Gugen, Peter Small had suggested that the growth of the sport would best be served by the BSAC forming branches rather than becoming a loose association of local clubs. The idea was approved and the original club in London was re-formed into the first branch, the London Branch. The second branch was then formed in East Lancashire and the third and fourth at Bristol and Blackpool. Each branch member was also a member of the new national club. Peter Small who had become the first national secretary also edited *Neptune*. The club continued to grow steadily. The system of individual membership meant that half the annual subscription was sent by the branches to the Club's Committee who in return provided a copy of the BSAC Diving Manual to each member together with regular issues of the magazine, soon renamed *Triton*. The part of each member's subscription kept by the branch was used to finance the purchase of aqualungs and other equipment.

The British Sub-Aqua Club was recognised as the governing body for the sport by the Central Council for Physical Recreation in 1955, and by the spring of 1956 the membership was nearly 2000. The training programme was well established and branches qualified their members as Third or Second Class divers – First Class being granted by national examination. In 1957 the Club formed its first overseas branch in Jamaica, and in 1958 Oscar Gugen relinquished the chairmanship of the Club to George Brookes so as to devote himself to the formation of an international organisation. By the end of the year the Club had 3000 members and 65 branches. Throughout the country these branches were helping local authorities, police and museums with projects ranging from the recovery of bodies to replacing sluice valves in reservoirs. The aqualung had become a working tool as well as a means of enjoying the underwater world. In 1959 Alan Broadhurst, who succeeded Jack Atkinson as the club's diving officer, formed the first federation of BSAC branches, NORFED.

In 1960 Colin McLeod who had been Vice-Chairman in the early days of the Club became Chairman and in 1962 organised a highly successful World Congress for the new World Federation at which Cousteau presented a lecture in which he looked forward to the time when gills might be grafted on to men. Sadly, during this period Peter Small lost his life while diving to 300m (1000ft) in an experiment organised by Dr Hannes Keller which is described in a later chapter. From 1963 to 1969 the club was led by Harry Gould who consolidated its position and initiated new appointments which were to have far reaching effects. With the financial aid of the Sports Council a full time national coach was appointed and the administration of the club was handled by an administrative agent. In 1963 Don Shiers, one of the club's first training officers, formed an independent Aquatic Club to establish standards of instruction and instructors. BSAC was ready to choose its first full time director who was provided with an office by the Sports Council and who was to be responsible for the consolidation and successful expansion of the club and the sport. At the same time the work of the national coach was taken over by nine part-time regional coaches, led by a part-time national coach. The Aquatic Club, which now included a number of branches, came back into the BSAC 'fold' as the Aquatic Federation in 1973. In the years that followed these appointments club membership rose sharply from 9000 members in 1968, to 11,000 in 1969 and 13,000 in 1970. The British Sub-Aqua Club had become the biggest single diving club in the world.

West Germany

Dr Hans Hass had a great influence on the development of sport diving in Germany even before the advent of the aqualung. The first club was formed in 1950 in Munich followed shortly afterwards by others in Hamburg and Berlin. In 1954 the Barakuda diving equipment company and the first club in Hamburg together started an underwater magazine, *Delphin*. At an exhibition in Dusseldorf in the same year a demonstration of diving was organised in a glass tank and following this more and more clubs were formed. In 1954, too, the official Germal Federation, VDST, was formed at Dusseldorf and *Delphin* became its official organ.

Scandinavia
The aqualung spread northwards to Scandinavia where the Finnish Federation of Diving Clubs was formed in 1956, the Norwegian *Dykkerforbund* in 1957 and the Swedish Federation in 1958.

The first underwater club in Denmark, the *Skovshoved Undersoiske Gruppe* had been formed slightly earlier in 1954. Its members used primitive home-made equipment until the arrival of the aqualung. The five or six existing clubs came together in 1965 to form the Danish Sportsdiving Federation, largely to prevent the passing of a law by the Danish Parliament to outlaw spearfishing.

Spearfishing
In many countries divers were obsessed with the new sport of spearfishing which developed from the early efforts of Gilpatric on the French Riviera and was normally practised without an aqualung, the use of which was felt to be unfair to the fish. In spite of a strong conservation movement in recent years there is no doubt that spearfishing using just the 'basic' equipment of mask, fins, tube and a simple spear or speargun, provided a really tough and adventurous sport which gave participants stamina in the water and a unique knowledge of the sea and its larger inhabitants. It was an important part of the history of diving. Unfortunately it has resulted in some species of fish being harder to find within diving depth in some regions, and the activity thus became unpopular with the increasing number of conservation minded aqualung enthusiasts.

USA
The first spearfishing club in the United States was the Bottom Scratchers formed under Glen Orr as long ago as 1933 following Gilpatric's articles in the *Saturday Evening Post*. It was somewhat select, however, as by the time that spearfisherman Wally Potts joined it in 1939 he became only the sixth member! Diving equipment in those days was limited to leaky and uncomfortable imported Japanese masks, but soon Potts and his 'buddy', Jack Prodanovich, were designing and building their own spears, goggles, face masks and even underwater sleds. They dived out of La Jolla, California,

which must be the cradle of American skindiving, using the original Owen Churchill fins.

The aqualung appeared in the United States as early as 1949 when Conrad Limbaugh introduced one at the Scripps Institute of Oceanography in California. In 1950 Cousteau brought the first supplies aboard the SS *Liberté*. The sport spread like wildfire and Southern California soon had the highest number of divers per head of population. By 1955, 25,000 aqualungs had been sold worldwide, 80% in California. The USA had more divers than any other country in the world and 'skindiving' became the fastest growing sport there.

Californian waters were comparatively cold and in 1950 Bradner and Bascom developed a 'wet' suit there. American divers were not slow to utilise them and by the mid 1950s were already diving on such exciting wrecks as the *Andrea Doria*, 55m (180ft) down in the open Atlantic. They also discovered the underwater paradise of the Bahamas. The sport was serviced by a lively magazine, *Skindiver*, which had existed since 1951. Its first diving editors were James Auxier and Charles Blakeslee. The magazine has been a considerable influence ever since.

In 1954 the Council for National Co-operation in Aquatics examined the safety aspects of the sport and assembled material which was used in a first 100-hour course for dive leaders in the following year. The YMCA was actively involved and Bernard Empleton of the Washington YMCA headed a committee to publish the material. It appeared in 1957 as *The Science of Skin and SCUBA Diving* and quickly became the best known and used text-book. The 'Y' set up its national training programme in 1959 and certified its first instructors in that year.

At first the 'club system' was widespread in the USA, but as the sales of equipment grew a new phenomenon, the 'dive shop' began to spread. Most shops had an attendant 'pro' instructor whose job, besides coaching, was to sell the equipment.

The Underwater Society of America had been formed 1959 encompassing many divers and diving organisations but the real force in American diving, apart from the commercial influence of the huge manufacturing and retailing companies, was to become that of the new instructor organisations.

In 1958 one of the many instructors, Neil Hess, began to run a section in *Skindiver* called 'The Instructors Corner'. Teachers wrote in with details of their 'programmes' and comments which were assessed before their names were added to a register of instructors. There seemed to be a need for a recognised course and examination. The

NAUI (National Association of Underwater Instructors) was born, becoming the official instructor training arm of the Underwater Society of America. NAUI was registered as a non-profit, educational corporation of professional underwater instructors and its motto became 'Safety Through Education'. It aimed to bring safe training to the vast number who were taking up the sport. The Association certified its own instructors through a six day course and examination.

NAUI is governed by a Board of Directors elected by the members, and has regional branches each with a branch manager. in 1969 the Board of Directors appointed the first full-time General Manager, responsible for its headquarters operation and the function of its branch managers. NAUI spread to Japan and Canada and in 1972 became the representative of the United States on the World Federation's Technical Committee. An annual 'IQ' (ICUE, International Conference on Underwater Education) is organised and by 1974 these conferences organised by Arthur Ullrich, general manager at that time, were attracting experts on training from all parts of the world. NAUI has now trained over 700,000 divers, certifying over 65,000 in 1977 alone.

The Professional Association of Diving Instructors (PADI) was formed in 1966 initially to provide diver training in the Mid-West of the USA and the Great Lakes area. Membership was obtainable on the strength of other recognised instructor qualifications and also through a PADI 'Instructors Institute'. The consequent exchange of information is published through PADI's *Undersea Journal*.

NASDS (The National Association of Skin Diving Schools) certifies instructors who are usually closely linked with dive shops and the sale of equipment. One of the most highly regarded instructor training organisations is that of the Los Angeles County whose programme is comprehensive and long-term.

Unfortunately, but perhaps inevitably, this split development resulted in relations between the rival instructor organisations becoming strained from time to time, under the fierce competition. However all sides came together to oppose restrictive legislation introduced in Los Angeles during recent years.

All instructors in the USA are permitted to qualify basic divers and issue them with a 'C' (Certification) Card which they then obtain from the parent organisation. The 'C' Card is very basic qualification and some holders may have had very little open water experience. Those holding it should continue their training and diving with more experienced divers and instructors. In recent years advanced SCUBA and instructor qualifications have been introduced by most of these organisations and lead to more continuation training. NAUI's headquarters is in Colton, California (see Appendix) and most of the other large organisations are based there, among the largest population of divers.

Canada

Canadians returning from World War 2 also brought diving equipment back from Europe and as early as 1950 a few were getting together to go diving with equipment imported from California. In the early 1950s clubs such as The Underwater Club of Canada began to operate and to train divers. Leaders such as Ben Davis saw the necessity for standardized training and in 1958 he, together with Steve Kozak and others formed the Ontario Underwater Council. Other Provinces followed suit. In 1961 the Ontario Council contacted NAUI in the USA to obtain support and instruction for an instructor certification course which was held at the University of Toronto. The co-operation resulted in Ben Davis being elected to the Board of Directors of NAUI. In the interests of standardisation, Ontario contacted the other provinces and in 1964 the Association of Canadian Underwater Councils (ACUC) was formed.

Ben Davis feels that the sport in Canada has gained through the encouragement and assistance it received from the Underwater Society of America, the British Sub-Aqua Club and particularly in recent years from the NAUI.

The influence of the USA has been a strong one and the system of dive shops, with professional instructors belonging to one of the major North American instructor agencies, has spread fast. By 1978 NAUI Canada under the leadership of Britton Mockridge was certifying 10,000 divers a year.

Australia

The sport in Australia began with spearfishing and spearfishing involvement has been strong ever since. The Underwater Spearfishermen's Association was formed in 1947 and was the forerunner of today's Australian Underwater Federation (AUF). The growth of aqualung diving dictated the change of name in 1966 and dive shops then began to appear although there was no formal instruction available.

In 1977 the Scuba Divers' Federation of Australia was formed to develop aqualung diving and to oppose excessive spearfishing. The SDFA now represents more SCUBA divers than any other organisation. The AUF, which is affiliated to the World Underwater Federation (CMAS) issues CMAS international certificates through instruction with the Federation of Australian Underwater Instructors (FAUI). A single Australian body to encompass all these functions has been suggested and would certainly simplify the administration of the sport.

There are two successful magazines, *Skindiving in Australia* (edited by Barry Andrewartha) and a quarterly newspaper called *Dive News*, edited by Peter Stone. Diver education is provided by the two national organisations as well as the partnership of editors Andrewartha and Stone who run the annual Oceans Underwater Congress and Film Festival in Melbourne.

Australia possesses some of the most beautiful diving locations in the world off its 20,000km (12,500 miles) of coastline. Most visiting divers head for the Great Barrier Reef which has a number of successful dive resorts, particularly Heron island in the south of the reef area. Many fascinating wrecks have been found such as the remains of Matthew Flinder's ships and the *Batavia*, an East Indiaman wrecked off Western Australia. There are approximately 60,000 divers in Australia, about 20,000 using SCUBA and less than half of these belong to clubs.

The best known divers in Australia are Ron and Valerie Taylor, Ben Cropp, Walt and Jean Deas, Steve Parish and Neville Coleman. The exploits of the Taylors are known worldwide through their exciting films and their participation in such expeditions as the search for the great white shark filmed under the title *Blue Water, White Death*. Ben Cropp is an ex-spearfisherman who has produced a number of films and books as have Walt and Jean Deas running the Heron Island resort. Walt is one of the world's best known underwater photographers. Steve Parish and Neville Coleman are authors, naturalists and underwater photographers.

South Africa

In South Africa too the main emphasis in the early years was on spearfishing and national spearfishing championships were started in 1956. The South African Underwater Union, formed in 1966, now represents the 'provincial' underwater unions and their member clubs. Activities include aqualung diving, spearfishing, underwater photography and underwater hockey. Wrecks also abound in South African waters and in recent years more and more have been found and charted by divers.

Diving Schools

In the early years of the sport the *Club Mediterrannée*, a French holiday organisation, had opened diving schools at a number of their strawhutted 'villages' in the Mediterranean. Together these schools soon formed the biggest professional aqualung diving school in the world. Their instructors, qualified by the French Federation, became known worldwide. They included Marcel Contal and Guy Poulet from France and Barry Blair, Peter Gill and Roger Bruce from England.

A number of Britons also ran their own schools off Mediterranean shores following the early pioneering work of Jack Atkinson. These included Pat and Joan Harrison at San Feliu in the Costa Brava; Peter Dick, Brian Hesketh and Mike Busuttili in Malta; Rowena Kerr on the Costa Blanca and the author at Giglio in Italy and Zembra in Tunisia.

The BSAC did not at this time provide instructor qualification that was nationally examined and recognised and so, a new British diving institution, The National Underwater Instructors Association (NUIA) was formed to run a national instructors examination based broadly on the French Federation Standards. The first examination was held in 1965 and soon afterwards the association's drive for international recognition of its qualifications led to the creation by the World Federation of a system of 'equivalents' which recognised the standards of instructors and divers in member countries. The NUIA and its examination were happily incorporated into the BSAC in 1969 together with a new series of BSAC instructor standards.

World Underwater Federation

The World Underwater Federation or CMAS (*Confédération Mondiale des Activites Sub-Aquatiques*) which has been referred to several times had been founded 1959 in Monaco by representatives of 15 countries and with Cousteau as president. It was composed of properly constituted and recognised national federations whose representatives met every 18 months at a General Assembly. Between these times an elected Executive Bureau works on more pressing and immediate problems. The World Federation was originally set up with two main committees—Sports and Technical. Luigi Ferraro, the Italian ex-frogman, became president of the Sports Committee and Oscar Gugen managed the Technical Committee. The more popular of these in the early years was the Sports Committee through which the annual World Spearfishing Championships were organised. Later the Technical Committee, which dealt with aqualung diving and techniques became more influential, especially after the establishment of the

Table 1   SPORTS DIVING STANDARDS

UK Standard	World Underwater Federation (CMAS) Standard	USA Standard
BSAC Sport Diver or E&F' diver	1 Star Diver	NAUI Junior Scuba Diver YMCA Bronze Star Diver
BSAC 3rd Class Diver	2 Star Diver	NAUI Basic Scuba Diver NAUI Sport Scuba Diver YMCA Silver Star Diver
BSAC 2nd Class Diver	3 Star Diver	NAUI Advanced Scuba Diver YMCA Gold Star Diver
BSAC 1st Class Diver	4 Star Diver	
BSAC Club Instructor	1 Star Instructor	YMCA Scuba Teaching Assistant
BSAC Advanced Instructor	2 Star Instructor	NAUI Underwater Instructor YMCA Assistant Instructor
BSAC National Instructor	3 Star Instructor	YMCA Scuba Instructor

international standards and the production of the World Federation certificates and cards which are now used and recognised throughout the world.

Jacques Dumas of France who was the General Secretary of the World Federation in the early years succeeded Cousteau as President in 1973. A Scientific Committee was formed in 1970. The headquarters of the organisation is currently in Paris.

Taking up the sport

Most diving clubs throughout the world expect a basic swimming standard from those who wish to take up the sport. The BSAC's swimming test consists of swimming 200m (219yds) freestyle and 100m (109yds) backstroke, swimming 50m (55yds) with a weight belt of 5kilos (11lb), floating on the back for 5 minutes, treading water for one and recovering six objects from the bottom of the swimming pool. It is not a speed test.

In a diving club every member should be able to help another in an emergency. This is unlike the situation in the holiday diving school where the professional instructor takes responsibility and so less initial ability is required and the beginner may be trained successfully under more controlled conditions. Holiday diving schools often aim to provide a quick and safe basic training course and some interesting holiday diving as an introduction to the sport. They then advise the holidaymaker to return and join a diving club for further training.

Diving schools may also exist outside the holiday sphere and cater for the person who needs a full-time course leading to a national diving certificate, but who has not the time to go through a standard club training. Such 'recognised schools' can provide this elementary training which can also, of course, save the time of the holidaymaker who wants to explore on every dive after arrival. In Great Britain a number of these schools are staffed by properly qualified BSAC instructors and may award BSAC qualification.

Training

Those thinking of taking up the sport should seek expert tuition, either through the recognised national federation and its clubs, or through recognised schools with qualified instructors. The BSAC now has over 1000 branches, not only in England, Scotland, Wales and Northern Ireland, but in 27 other countries. Lists are available from their headquarters.

In the United States beginners should check the qualifications of the diving instructor whose course they are thinking of joining. He should have been qualified by one of the major instructor agencies. Above all, never learn from a diving friend. Although friends may be competent divers themselves they can easily forget to give some of the vital knowledge that could mean the difference between life and death.

As mentioned previously, learning to dive as part of a holiday can be a pleasant introduction to the sport, and many enthusiasts began this way under the careful eye of a qualified diving school instructor. Remember, though, that it may be difficult for a diving school to provide a qualification in the time available and that, if you join a club or course before leaving you might enjoy your holiday diving that much more. Clubs or courses near home can qualify the beginner providing that successful progress is made through the training

1 John Lethbridge's diving apparatus, 1715 was used successfully by the inventor on many wrecks.

2 Alexander Lambert used the first autonomous oxygen apparatus to close a door in the flooded Severn tunnel in 1880.

3 John Deane of Whitstable developed the first diving helmet about 1820. He worked on the wreck of the *Royal George* using a sloop, the *Mary*.

4 Edmund Halley, the astronomer, produced a successful diving bell in 1690. Fresh air came down in barrels and divers could work briefly outside the bell.

5 Early self-contained compressed air apparatus was developed in France by Benoit Rouquayrol and Auguste Denayrouze in 1865. It was called the Aerophore.

6 The Italian firm 'Sorima' used a simple observation tube nicknamed 'the eye' to direct salvage of gold from the *Egypt* in 1922.

7 The standard helmet and suit was widely used throughout the world from its introduction in the 1830s until the mid twentieth century.

8 During World War 2, Italian frogmen used a partly sunken ship the *Olterra* as a base for human torpedo attacks on Gibraltar.

9 Modern Sport Diver Badges: World Underwater Federation diver and instructor badges and cards (upper three) give evidence of comprehensive national training. British Sub Aqua Club instructors are nationally examined and qualified (lower three).

10 The largest training organisations are in the USA where there are three million divers (upper three). The French Federation instructors badge (lower).

11 Swedish instructor (top). German sport diver (lower left). Nordic snorkeller (lower right).

12 Lightweight 'wet' suits have revolutionised amateur diving.

13 The 'basic equipment' of modern sport divers – mask, fins and snorkel tube.

14 A 'snorkel diver' or 'snorkeller' uses this equipment to explore a reef.

15 Amateur divers excavating Britain's most famous historical wreck, the *Mary Rose* which sank in the Solent in 1545.

16 A diver on the wreck of the *Kennermerland* levers up a lead ingot.

17 Ducatoons brought up by the *Kennermerland* divers.

18 Underwater orienteering competitor at Fort Bovisand in Devon. Modern devices for this sport indicate direction, speed and distance travelled.

19 'Octopush' or underwater hockey is played in swimming pools without using the aqualung.

20 Amateur divers recovering part of a missing X-craft from Kaafjord inside the Arctic circle in 1974 using an inflatable lifting bag.

21 Diving spelaeologists adapt aqualung equipment to enable them to pass through
narrow passages into underground caves.

22 Some oceanic animals can be dangerous. A wary diver with jellyfish.

23 Men are often more dangerous to sharks than vice-versa.

24 Diver Maura Mitchell makes contact with a friendly wild dolphin in British waters.

25 Clown fish are not so friendly as they guard the anemone that gives them protection.

26 Queen angel fish are among the most beautiful inhabitants of coral reefs observed and photographed by divers.

27 The beautiful sea slugs or nudibranchs were considered rare until they were regularly seen by amateur divers.

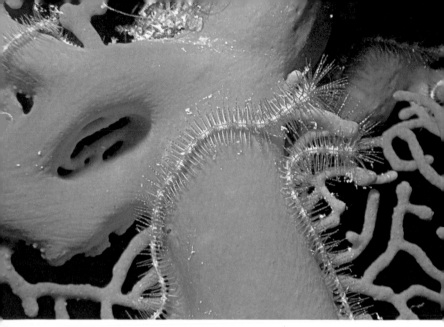

28 Close-up underwater photography shows the beauty of tropical reef inhabitants such as this brittle star deep on a Fijian reef.

29 Gorgonians or sea fans feed by extending tiny polyps.

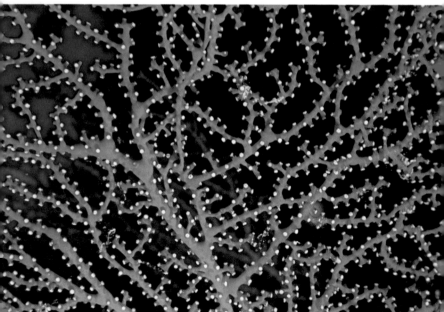

30 The Great Barrier Reef of Australia supports thousands of animals including these black corals and basket stars.

31 The diver's world is full of strange shapes and animals that look like plants.

32 Tunicates or sea squirts siphon small food particles from the sea.

33 A crinoid or feather star photographed at Heron Island against a background of gorgonia.

34 The beauty of the underwater world is demonstrated by this play of light on fishes under a pier.

35 An aqualung diver approaching a cave full of sponges.

36 A first night dive is an experience that is never forgotten.

37 Diving into the 'blue holes' of caves in the Bahamas was pioneered by Dr George Benjamin.

38 HRH Prince Charles, President of the British Sub Aqua Club, dives under the ice in the Canadian arctic with Dr Joe McInnes.

39 Exploration of shallow wrecks can be done with just snorkel, mask and fins.

40 One of the most beautiful wrecks in the world – the *Umbria* off Port Sudan.

41 Jean Deas on the wreck of the *Cooma* in Australian waters.

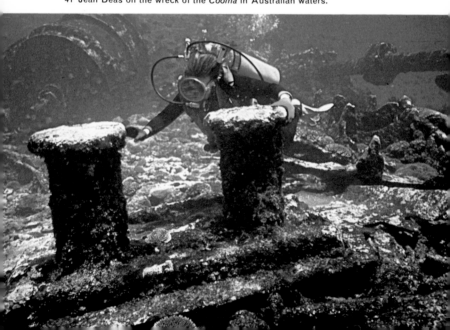

42 The modern sport diver wears an adjustable buoyancy life jacket and a weight belt
to counter the buoyancy of his wet suit. The demand valve gives easy breathing
from the air cylinder. A knife, depth gauge and watch are carried.

43 The bathyscaphe *Trieste* piloted by Jacques Piccard and Donald Walsh reached the deepest part of the ocean, 10.900 m (35,800 ft) in 1958.

44 George Bass of the University of Pennsylvania brought the science of underwater archaeology to new heights with his detailed excavation of ancient wrecks off Turkey.

45 Submersible decompression chambers which allow a diver to be delivered to and from the seabed have been used for many years.

46 British Military Diving Badges: Army Compressed Air Diver badge (top left). Royal Navy Seaman (Diver) Badge (top right). Royal Navy Leading Seaman (Diver) Badge (bottom left). Royal Navy Petty Officer (Diver) Badge (bottom right).

47 The American, Ed Link was the first to organise an underwater living experiment in 1962. He used Robert Stenuit, a Belgian as his aquanaut.

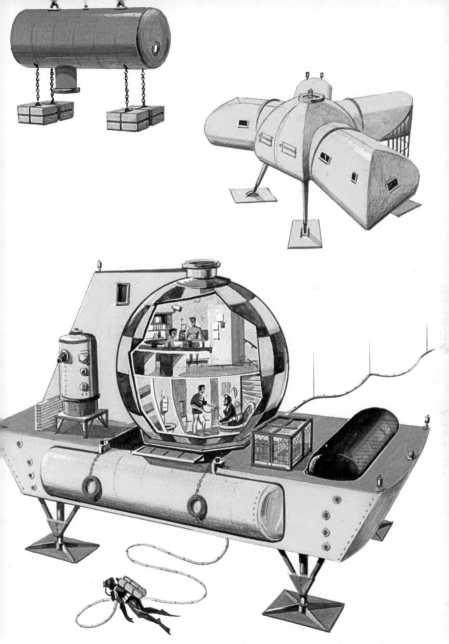

48 Jacques Cousteau also organised underwater houses in which French aquanauts lived for long periods. *Conshelf I* was a simple tube, while *Conshelf II* (Starfish House) and *Conshelf III* were considerably more sophisticated.

49 In the US Navy's *Sealab II* experiment in 1965, aquanauts (including astronaut Scott Carpenter) lived underwater for 10 days at a depth of 63 m (205 ft).

50 *Tektite II* underwater habitat was established in the Virgin Islands and studies were made of sea life. A diver brings a lobster to show to his partner in the dome of the underwater house.

51 A member of the crew of *Tektite I* relaxes during his stay in 1969.

52 A commercial diver wearing a Kirby Morgan band mask.

53 In difficult conditions, commercial divers use lightweight helmets such as the Aquadyne model. Voice communication can be maintained.

54 A diver practising underwater cutting during a course run by the Society for Underwater Technology at Fort Bovisand in Devon

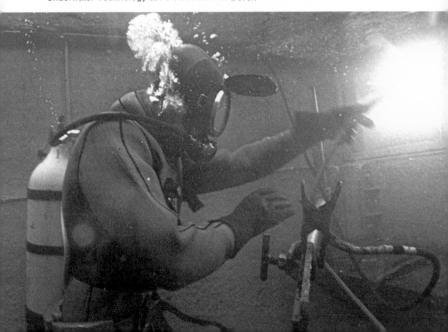

55 Swindell helmets are used by civil engineering divers descending into docks and rivers.

56 In low visibility conditions, divers are lowered on a stage which helps to position
and orientate them more easily.

57 A diver being prepared on the *Glomar IV* oil rig.

58 A North Sea diver descending to work in a cage wearing a Kirby Morgan band mask.

59 North Sea divers working on 'umbilicals' out of a modern bell repair a pipeline.

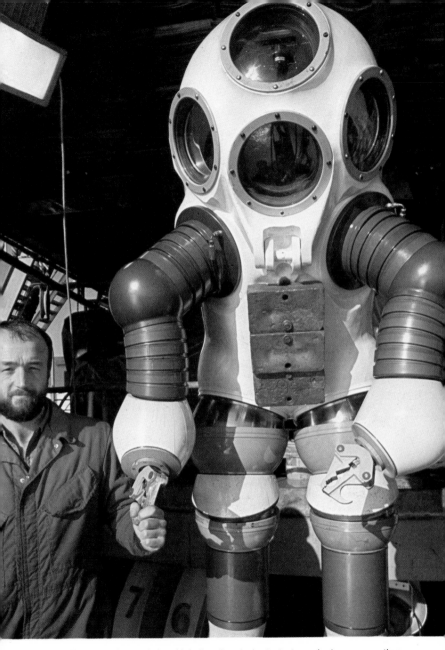

60 JIM, the modern suit in which the diver is kept at atmospheric pressure thus avoiding decompression and other problems.

61 An underwater oil terminal of the future.

programme. A national award such as the BSAC 'Elementary' or 'Sports Diver' Certificate or a NAUI, PADI or YMCA 'C' card course will give confidence and a good grounding in the sport.

The swimming test is not a race, but checks that the potential diver is at home and competent in the water. Training then usually continues in a swimming pool where the new diver gains confidence with the unfamiliar equipment.

Training is provided cheaply by local clubs or branches who meet at pools for one or two training evenings each week. Weekend dives are then organised to the sea or inland open water areas. Film shows, lectures and other social events are usually part of the programme of every diving club and help to make this a most enjoyable way of taking up the sport.

Basic Equipment

After the swimming test the diver must master the 'basic equipment' of face mask, foot fins and 'snorkel' tube.

The fins, which are used in a wide, slow crawl kick, provide the propulsion, and leave the divers hands free to be used for holding other equipment or investigating the sea bed. They should fit comfortably and have a fairly flexible blade. The mask provides clear vision underwater. Without it, objects would appear blurred, as our eyes are designed to see in air. The mask should cover the eyes and nose, the single pane preventing the double vision that comes with goggles and it should be possible to blow air into it through the nose when necessary. Modern masks also feature indentations which allow the diver to squeeze the nose through the mask and thus 'compensate' or equalise the pressure on the ears. The snorkel tube provides a means of easy breathing through the mouth while lying weighted on the surface, without the need to turn the head to the side.

It is essential to become as competent as possible with these three items of diving equipment. When divers can swim strongly with them they should be able to 'swim their way out of trouble' whether or not they are also wearing an aqualung.

Some decide to stay with this basic equipment and become 'snorkellers' exploring the sea floor on short breath-holding forays. If you decide to take up spearfishing it will probably be at this stage and using this equipment plus a speargun. Remember though that, as already mentioned, some species of fish are becoming hard to find in some parts of the world so a check should be made with your club or instructor first.

Professor Hans and Lotte Hass

Captain Jacques Cousteau

Professor Jacques Piccard

Commandant Phillipe Tailliez

Maître Jacques Dumas

Doctor Joe McInnes

Colin McLeod

Oscar Gugen

Suits

Once the snorkeller goes out into open water, whether in an inland lake or sea a 'wet' suit will soon be needed to protect against the cold and from sharp rocks and 'spiky' animals. In principle the wet suit lets in a little water but this soon warms up to body heat. In practice, with a well-fitting suit, very little water will find its way in. The wet suit, unlike the traditional frogman's 'dry' suit, does not suffer from the disadvantage of air being squeezed in its (and the diver's) extremities. It is thus comparatively comfortable to wear.

There are also 'variable volume', or 'inflatable' dry suits which are warm, comfortable and dry but which are more complicated to use and much more expensive to buy. They are used by divers who are spending long periods in cold water.

Other Equipment

Once the diver has a wet suit a weight belt and weights will also be needed to allow readjustment for excess bouyancy. The belt should have an easily operated 'quick release' and should be worn so that it falls away from the diver in an emergency.

A lifejacket is a very useful buy. Surface life jackets will keep a diver afloat on the surface where most initial difficulties are likely to occur, but will not operate efficiently at depth. Experienced aqualung divers thus favour the more expensive 'adjustable buoyancy life jackets'(ABLJs) which are known as 'buoyancy compensators' in the United States. These contain a small bottle of compressed air which can be filled from an aqualung before a dive, and will inflate the jacket to bring up the diver from depth in an emergency.

It is essential to wear a depth gauge and timing device.

Duck Diving

The technique of snorkel or 'duck' diving begins when you are lying flat on the surface and breathing through the snorkel tube. You then take a deep breath, bend downwards from the waist and allow your feet to rise out of the water. This puts you into a vertical downward glide. As splashing on the surface is inefficient and may disturb the fish, the fins are not used until the glide has reached a point where the feet are below the surface. Slow wide strokes then push you steeply downwards. A squeeze of your nose, together with a 'blow' and your ears clear, and you arrive on the bottom. A check on your depth gauge gives confidence. Soon it is time to return. The snorkel tube has now filled with water, although air pressure in the mouth has kept it out of the throat. When the snorkel breaks surface the last of the air is blown out, thus clearing it of water for the next breath.

Snorkelling Hazards

Snorkelling might seem an easy pastime, with simple equipment and few hazards. It is essential to know what these are, however, and how to deal with them.

Pain in the ears when going down is caused by water pressure distorting the eardrum inwards. By holding the nose and blowing gently against the pressure air can be passed through the eustachian tube to the other side of the eardrum. The pressure is then equalised, the pain disappears and the diver can continue downwards.

The mask can press in on the face, either because of the pressure of the water increasing on descent or, more often, because the diver has inadvertently breathed in through the nose. This should be corrected by blowing a little air out through the nose to adjust the pressure.

Snorkellers frequently suffer from cold as they are not limited by the amount of air that they have with them and are often engrossed with the activities of the fish below. They should never stay until they are shivering in the water. The sea which can develop unpredictable currents and sudden squalls must always be respected. All the local information should be obtained before leaving the beach.

In Britain a BSAC Snorkeller's Award for juniors was introduced by Alex Double together with a snorkel instructor's certificate for teachers. Under the influence of Lionel Blandford, an enthusiastic club instructor, a National Snorkellers Club was set up and has already introduced over 10,000 youngsters from 9 to 15 to the sport. Many branches of this BSAC junior club exist and holidays are organised in Britain and abroad.

Underwater Competitions

Although snorkelling is mainly taken up as part of the preliminary training for aqualung diving, snorkellers can also take part in competitive activities which have become more developed in recent years.

Spearfishing was the first competitive underwater activity. Since 1954 World Championships have been organised by the World Federation and hosted by different member nations. The size of fish caught has been extraordinary and spearfishermen have improved their technique over the years until they are able to fish 30m (100ft) down while breath-holding.

More recently, a number of specialists have set depth records without the aqualung culminating in a dive to 100m (330ft) by yoga expert Jacques Mayol in 1976. There is some doubt, however, as to how much pressure the human body can resist when lungs are filled with air at atmospheric pressure, and for this and other reasons such records have not been encouraged by the World Federation.

Depth records with the aqualung were also attempted in the early days of the sport but these proved even more dangerous. Maurice Fargues a compatriot of Cousteau, died at 120m (395ft) and Hope Root, an American lawyer, somewhat deeper. The cause of death was almost certainly nitrogen narcosis, a form of 'depth drunkenness', and even though these attempts have been likened to putting one's head in a gas oven, turning on the gas and seeing how long one can retain one's consciousness, there are still occasionally misguided attempts of this sort.

The first attempt to swim the English Channel underwater was made by an American, Jane Baldasare, in 1960. She swam close to the surface inside a 6m (20ft) cage that was towed by the supporting fishing boat. Her backup team from the BSAC's London Branch included Harry Gould, Mike Busuttili, Byron Cowie and Chris Whittaker. They passed down aqualungs as needed but bad weather and an equipment fault defeated her. Her second attempt in 1961 was managed by Don Shiers but was also unsuccessful due to bad weather. Her husband, Fred Baldasare, became the first successful underwater swimmer to cross in 1962 taking 18 hours for the swim.

Later that year Byron Cowie nearly became the first Englishman to complete the swim but had to give up only 13km (8 miles) from the British coast when his team of helpers became sea sick! At the end of the summer Simon Paterson, an English teenager also managed by Shiers, used an 'airline rig' to cross in the record time of 13 hours 50 minutes. Fred Baldasare went on to swim the Straits of Messina and the Straits of Gibraltar underwater.

Finswimming

In 1960 the first international finswimming competitions were organised. Competitors race along the surface using fins and the sport is normally organised in olympic-sized pools. The technique has been particularly developed in the Eastern European countries and in the USSR. Over the years the size of the fins used in these competitions has grown and some top participants now even put both feet in one enormous triangular fin and use a dolphin kick. The results are spectacular. The world record for 100m (109yds) was held in 1978 by Andrey Owsaynikow of the USSR in a time of 41.5 seconds. His compatriot, Wladimir Malinin, covered 1500m (1640yds) in 13 minutes 50 seconds. In 1979 Russian Raisa Gourskaia became the ladies 100m champion with a time of 45.3 seconds and her team mate Tatiana Petchatnova covered 1500m in 14 minutes 16 seconds. Although these competitions attract amateur club divers in the West, participants in World Championships are sometimes ex-champion swimmers who have little knowledge of diving and the aqualung.

In 1979 a young Frenchman, Daniel Mainguy, swam from Cherbourg to Swanage wearing a wet suit and fins. Battling against conflicting currents and rough seas he took 38 hours to cover the 145km (90 miles).

Underwater Techniques

It is necessary, however, to be an aqualung diver to take part in the next competitive activity which is known as underwater techniques or underwater orienteering. The underwater technique competitions involve navigation underwater and some speed swimming with the aqualung. International championships are organised by the World Underwater Federation and in this field, too, sophisticated equipment has been developed by the USSR and Eastern European countries. Their competitors swim with a specially prepared panel of instruments which record not only direction but also speed and distance.

Underwater Hockey

The most recent development in the international competitive field has been in the area of true underwater games. In the BSAC a form of underwater hockey called Octopush has been played since the early 1950s. A lead puck or 'squid' is pushed along the bottom of the pool towards goals at the ends. Divers use basic equipment returning to the surface to breathe. In 1972 a national 'ladder' was started and in 1976 the British Octopush Association came into being to organise championships becoming part of the BSAC in 1978.

Interest gradually grew in underwater games, and the World Federation decided to set up a commission to organise them and to arrange international championships. At the inaugural meeting at Fort Bovisand near Plymouth it was reported that Germany and the Scandanavian countries also played 'underwaterball' or 'underwater rugby' which was another swimming pool game but played in three dimensions using a water-filled ball thrown through the water and into nets similar to those used in basketball.

International rules for underwater hockey and rugby have now been formulated and agreed under the chairmanship of Alan Bax of Great Britain the President of the Commission. These new games are particularly useful in fostering contacts between divers of different clubs and countries and in increasing a diver's stamina and fitness.

Aqualung Diving
Most snorkellers will sooner or later want to go on to try the aqualung which has the enormous fascination of providing long periods on the bottom, and the thrill of the sensation of being weightless during underwater flight. It has been aptly described by Cousteau as the 'passport to inner space'.

To learn the techniques of aqualung or SCUBA diving the snorkeller should be in good health and have reached the age of 14. A competent instructor is also needed. One of the great advantages of the aqualung is that it allows divers to breathe their air at the same pressure as the water through which they are swimming. They therefore never suffer from the massive 'squeezes' that sometimes affected helmet divers. The human body, being largely composed of water, is virtually incompressible. Pressure does, however, affect the air in the lungs and small cavities behind the ears and in the sinuses.

The breathing of compressed air brings other complications, though. The 79% of nitrogen in atmospheric air begins to dissolve under pressure in the diver's blood and fatty tissues. Little harm is caused as long as the diver takes enough time on the ascent to prevent the formation of nitrogen bubbles due to rapid changes of pressure. The development of 'decompression tables' by Haldane has been described and first gave an indication as to the length of time it is possible to stay at each depth and when it was necessary to make decompression stops near the surface to eliminate excess nitrogen.

The Dangers of Aqualung Diving
Most amateur divers complete their dives within the 'no-stop' times so that stops are unnecessary. However, divers should always return slowly to the surface, never overtaking their own small exhaust bubbles. Divers who break these rules may suffer from the 'bends' or decompression sickness which can cause pain, paralysis or even death, depending on where the bubbles lodge in the body. The best cure is to rush the divers to the nearest recompression chamber where they can be rapidly pressurised again inside and then very slowly 'decompressed' until all the symptoms have disappeared and they can be returned to surface pressure again   At greater depths divers will suffer from nitrogen narcosis, an effect on the brain resulting in slow thinking, apprehension and confusion. This is also described as depth

116

drunkenness, and more poetically by the French as 'Rapture of the Great Depths'. In the less poetic Royal Navy it has always been referred to as 'the narcs' and stiff-lipped sailors were often loath to report its symptoms and effects. Nitrogen narcosis is particularly dangerous to aqualung divers who are dependent on keeping their breathing mouthpieces in place with their teeth and on swimming and calculating on the bottom. The easy cure is a return to a higher level where the symptoms disappear, leaving no after effects.

The aqualung provides air 'on demand' to the diver, each breath is thus provided at the same pressure as the surrounding water. Because of this the diver must not hold his breath when swimming up to the surface; otherwise the air in the lungs will expand with the drop in the surrounding pressure, causing eventual rupture of the lungs. This is a serious condition generally known as air embolism. In the unlikely event of a complete air failure therefore the diver should either share another diver's aqualung or return to the surface breathing out all the way up.

In spite of these dangers aqualung diving is one of the safest of sports and the equipment is extremely reliable. The accidents that do occur are usually due to diver thoughtlessness or to changing weather conditions.

The Aqualung
The modern breathing set has three main components; a cylinder of compressed air, a demand valve, which includes a mouthpiece for breathing, and a harness to attach them to the diver's back. In the United States cylinders are generally known as 'tanks' and the demand valve as the 'regulator'.

The cylinders are constructed of steel or aluminium, and are designed to contain pure breathing air at pressure of 150 to 200 atmospheres.

The demand valve reduces the air pressure coming from the cylinder and supplies it as required.

The harness consists of two shoulder straps to attach the breathing set to the diver's back and a strap round the waist or between the legs to stabilise it.

The exhaled air rises through the water in large flattened bubbles and these can often be followed on the surface in calm weather. This is the main reason why the aqualung is not used for military operations. Every aqualung should have a system to warn the diver when his air is getting low.

Modern sport divers in tidal waters was buoys to indicate their position to following inflatable boats. The blue and white international code 'A' flag indicates 'diver down'.

Techniques

In tidal waters sports divers often drift across the bottom holding a reel with a line to a small diver marker buoy on the surface.

A light diving boat can then follow this buoy and be in position to pick up the divers wherever and whenever they surface. The buoy and also the boat should show a reproduction of the international code 'A' flag which means 'I have a diver down, keep clear and at slow speed .

One of the secrets of succesful diving is to be able to relax, always keeping energy in reserve for a possible emergency. Over-exertion can lead to a build up of carbon dioxide and breathlessness. By carefully adjusting weights and other buoyancy factors a diver can become virtually weightless, a very pleasant sensation shared with astronauts. In fact, for this reason, aqualung diving is part of the obligatory astronaut training.

The trained diver can overcome most hazards and the apparatus is remarkably reliable and adaptable. If the air fails or has been completely used up, two divers can 'share' together passing one breathing mouthpiece between them and taking two breaths each.

If water leaks into his mask the diver turns on his back, presses his fingers against the top of his face plate and blows air through his nose. This excess air then blows any water out through the bottom, below the nose. One of the most important rules is 'never dive alone'. Each pair, or small group, of divers should have a recognised leader and communication underwater is by international hand signals.

Boat Diving
Larger diving boats are equipped with spacious ladders to allow divers to climb on board while still wearing fins but much sport diving is done from the smaller inflatables with outboard engines. The divers then travel, facing inwards, sitting on the inflatable sides and roll backwards into the sea for their dive. On their return they take off their aqualungs in the water and pass them up to the boat handler before scrambling aboard. Inflatables have proved very useful for the majority of divers who are based inland as they are easily transportable, seaworthy fast and manoeuverable. On a dive the boat handler will stay near the divers' buoys, positioning the boat near them should another boat approach too close and threaten to run over them.

Wrecks and Underwater Archaeology
Underwater swimming is not just a healthy and enjoyable sport in itself, giving the diver the opportunity to explore a virtually new world, but is also a means to engage in other more specialised activities such as underwater photography, archaeology or studies of animals and the marine environment. Not only have many ancient wrecks been located by amateur divers but they have also been subsequently excavated by them. Underwater archaeology needs responsible club divers and in Britain a diving archaeologist is usually assigned to advise such groups who are allowed to continue to survey and excavate their wreck under their guidance. Divers may attend underwater archaeology courses or join established teams on wrecks. The passing of the Protection of Wrecks act in Britain in 1973 made life easier for those investigating historic wrecks and wrecks of historical interested are now 'designated' by a government appointed committee and may then only be worked on by the finders under suitable supervision. Valuables from such wrecks may subsequently

be sold at auction, the proceeds going largely to those who have found and worked on them.

In other parts of the world the law may vary and divers, especially those finding treasure galleons, may have to engage in long negotiations with government agencies on the percentages that they may claim. Most profit goes to the government concerned giving less incentive to the divers to report their finds. Nearly every wreck belongs to someone. If not the original owners then the insurance company that has paid out on its losses, often to Lloyds of London or the Salvage Association. In Britain those salvaging casually must report their finds to the Receivers of Wreck who are situated at various points around the coast.

The *Mary Rose*

Britain's most famous wreck is the *Mary Rose* which turned turtle and went down in the Solent on 20 July 1545 while sailing out with a British fleet to intercept marauding French men-of-war. Her sinking was watched by King Henry VIII from Southsea Castle. His remarks at the time were not recorded! The *Mary Rose* was 46m (150ft) long with a 15m (50ft) beam, a unique Tudor battleship of new design. She went down with a Vice-Admiral and 700 men. She was found and worked on briefly by the Deane brothers (see Chapter 1) but was not heard of again thereafter. In 1965, however, an author and amateur diver, Alexander McKee, set out to find her using sonar which reached under the silt of the main shipping channel. Patience and persistance were rewarded by the discovery of the wreck 13m (43ft) below the surface and later of many objects used in everyday life. The *Mary Rose* is being worked on by amateur BSAC divers under the direction of Margaret Rule, a nautical archaeologist and is now to be completely recovered and placed in a museum at Portsmouth. This exciting project should come to fruition in 1982 when the remains of a whole cross section should be on show.

Some of the problems of preservation of a complete ship have already been succesfully tackled in Sweden where the *Wasa*, another ancient ship, was successfully raised from the bed of the harbour at Stockholm and is now housed in a magnificent museum.

Other Excavations

A number of British Sub-Aqua Club branches have carried out searches and excavations of such wrecks as HMS *Dartmouth*, sunk in the Sound of Mull in Scotland in 1690, and in recent years the first traces of Bronze Age wrecks have been found by the club's coaches and branches. The wreck of the *Kennermerland* has been found in the Shetlands and worked on by the BSAC's archaeological adviser Keith Muckelroy. Britain has more wrecks around her coast than any other country in the world and much remains to be done.

Besides ancient wrecks, some BSAC members have specialised in raising more recent vessels. Club members under the supervision of Peter Cornish, a regional coach, lifted a complete Beaufighter aircraft and later the remains of XE-8, a midget submarine, off Portland. The lifts are mainly executed using numbers of oil drums and lifting bags which are taken down empty and then filled with compressed air on the bottom to provide enormous lift.

In 1974 Peter Cornish led a 36 man expedition into the Arctic to look for the remains of X-5, the British midget submarine that had disappeared while attacking the 56,000 tonne German battleship *Tirpitz* in 1943 (chapter 2). Diving in near freezing conditions they discovered the remains of an X craft and raised it to the surface. The remains are now in the Imperial War Museum in London and the expedition proved that amateur divers could make unique contri-

Amateur divers using aqualungs have recovered wartime aircraft. This US Navy 'Hellcat' was recovered after 26 years in the sea off California.

butions to the historical record.

Underwater Spelaeology and Cave Diving
A small number of spelaeologists have specialised in diving through sumps, pools and underwater lakes. In 1922 Norbert Casteret carried out an amazing solo exploration of a cave at Montespan near Toulouse. He penetrated two miles into the cave, breath-hold diving through sumps, and found evidence that primitive man once lived there. In 1934 Balcombe and Sheppard had explored Swildon's Hole in Somerset and a cave diving group was formed in 1946 at Oxford. These early divers used oxygen or even helmets but with the advent of the aqualung compressed air was used. Spelaeological divers now normally mount one cylinder on each side at hip level which enables them to traverse narrow tunnels. Each cylinder has its own demand valve and the divers wear helmets with torches strapped to them. In 1978 British and German cave divers penetrated 900m (3000ft) through narrow tunnels into Keld Head, one of the Ingleton caves. The techniques of underwater spelaeology involve diving alone in hazardous conditions and participants are considered more as spelaeologists than as divers.

Diving is also undertaken in larger caves using more conventional sports diving equipment and techniques. Cousteau explored the Fountain of Vaucluse in 1946 nearly losing his life in the process. Diving has become popular in the Florida caves and under the influence of an intrepid and brilliant photographer, Dr George Benjamin, in the deep 'blue holes' of the Bahamas. In Australia divers have explored the 'Picaninny Ponds', deep fresh water caves in South Australia.

Underwater Photography
Only shortly after the invention of the camera itself, an Englishman named William Thompson took the world's first underwater photograph off the Weymouth coast in 1856. His leaking camera managed to record a passable, if somewhat dim image of sand and seaweed and though the result may not have been dramatic he had made a crucial contribution and underwater photography had been born.

In 1893 the French zoologist, Louis Boutan, who became known as the 'father of underwater photography' had used a wet plate camera sealed in a copper housing. It weighed over 400 pounds underwater and Boutan using a conventional helmet produced the first undersea flash photograph.

Underwater photography really became a practical proposition with the advent of the aqualung and miniature cameras. The camera is now an invaluable tool in the hands of the marine scientist or the creative artist. Few people are aware of the difficulties. The distance at which objects can be clearly distinguished is severely limited as water scatters light to such an extent that it is 2000 times less transparent than air. In the sea the scattering is further increased by microscopic particles of plankton, and visibility varies from zero in some harbours to over 60m (200ft) off tropical reefs. Underwater conditions are usually like a foggy day on land. Despite this, equipment and techniques can create an illusion of clarity in the final picture. As a rule it is better to get as close as possible to the subject so that the light has less distance to travel from the subject to the film. In low visibility this closeness may result in it no longer being possible to frame the whole subject in the view finder. Special wide angle lenses have been developed to solve this problem. Not only is light scattered by water but it is also absorbed. On the way down light intensity diminishes and the seven colours of the spectrum behave differently. Red, the colour with the longest wavelength, disappears only a few feet below the surface. Further down the blue-green colours predominate and the bright colours of a reef are hidden by a blue shroud. This can be dispelled by flash guns or floodlights and the film then records the true colours of the reef. Many scientific discoveries have been made by amateur undersea photographers who, sometimes unwittingly, record a new species of fish or coral.

It is now possible for any diver, even with a simple camera, to produce high quality underwater photographs. In Britain the 'British Society of Underwater Photographers' (BSUP) exists to encourage and develop the technique by exchange of ideas and production of a 'data book'. The society organises regular meetings, newsletters and competitions.

The coelacanth, a fish believed to have become extinct some 60 million years ago was discovered alive in the Indian Ocean and photographed in 1979 by underwater photographer Peter Scoones.

Underwater Holidays

There are a number of large travel organisations specialising in diving holidays and also numerous smaller centres. All provide the heavier equipment that is difficult to transport by air – cylinders and weight belts. They invariably have their own compressors and often diving boats to reach the most interesting locations. Some larger vessels are adapted for diving cruises. The dive guides should be qualified instructors or at least highly qualified divers. Diving holidays are now run in the Indian and Pacific Oceans, the Red Sea, the Caribbean and the Canaries as well as the Mediterranean. In the UK details of holidays are available from the BSAC holiday information officer c/o BSAC HQ. In the USA the diving magazines run many advertisements and the American Adventurers Association also features diving expeditions in their newsletter.

Undersea life

Amateur divers provide thousands of observant 'eyes under the sea'. Tiny, colourful sea slugs called nudibranchs were thought to be rare until amateur divers observed and collected them.

Another spectacular discovery by an amateur diver took place off the Island of Lundy in the Bristol Channel. A field course in marine biology for divers was being run by Doctor Keith Hiscock who has designated the area as an 'underwater nature reserve'. One of the students was curious about a number of burrows on the muddy bottom at a depth of 12m (40ft). What, if anything, was inside? There was only one way to find out. He wriggled his hand and arm down into a vertical hole up to his armpit and pulled out a writhing, eel-like fish. Its colours were astonishing – pink with mauve and green bands. It was identified as a red band fish (*Cepola rubescens*) that had never before been found in shallow water. Diving scientists then began a comprehensive study of the fish and new knowledge was gained.

Dr David Bellamy of Durham University was one of the first to realise the potential of thousands of aqualung divers in clubs around the country and used them succesfully in an number of studies of pollution around British coasts and also in Europe. The divers collected recognisable marine animals such as starfish and mussels which gave indications of the amount of toxic matter in the water. The specimens were sent to the University for analysis and provided the first comprehensive figures on pollution off British coasts. By 1978 amateur BSAC divers were taking part in dives as far afield as the Chagos archipelago in the middle of the Indian Ocean where a joint Forces/BSAC expedition studied these little known islands and reefs. The Underwater Conservation Society formed in 1979 now provides projects for divers and thousands of records have been made. The co-ordination and guidance of UCS is in the hands of a dedicated diving biologist, Dr Bob Earll.

The future for amateur diving is a bright one as the younger generation looks more and more towards the new exploration sports and especially this one that gives opportunities for discovery in a completely new world opened up to all for the first time in history.

124

4
20th Century Scientific, Police and Military Divers

The production of an efficient diving helmet by Deane and Siebe did not result in a rush of marine biologists to see the underwater world for themselves. The helmet became used by 'professionals' only and their stories of the 'denizens of the deep' were often less than accurate.

One exception was Henry Milne-Edwards, a French naturalist who rejected the normal technique of trawling and fishing. He made his first dive in Sicily in 1844 and was fascinated with the 'marvellous transparence' of the Mediterranean. Milne-Edwards used a simple open helmet to collect bottom animals from depths down to a mere 9m (30ft). Although a small number of scientists followed him, it was not until after the invention of the aqualung a hundred years later that they really began to study beneath the surface.

William Beebe and the Bathysphere
Another exception was William Beebe, although his work was chiefly in the deep sea beyond the level of helmet divers. Scientists in the nineteenth century knew little of the depth of the oceans until the laying of the first transatlantic telegraph cables provided an insight. However, naturalists like Edward Forbes researching in 1842 were still convinced that there was no life below a depth of 460m (1500ft). New expeditions were mounted to probe the deep sea bed. Professor Wyville Thomson recovered organisms from 1500m (5000ft) in 1868 and in the next year had trawled to a depth of 4387m (14,395ft). The Admiralty put a corvette HMS *Challenger*, at his disposal. In a voyage lasting nearly four years the *Challenger* made sensational discoveries and the new science of oceanography was born.

Beebe was a naturalist who had become fascinated with exploring the shallow West Indian coral reefs with a home-made helmet.

'When I first put on a diving helmet and climbed down the submerged ladder then I knew that I had added thousands upon thousands of miles of possible joy to my earthly life ... for personal exploration under the ocean is really unearthly, we're penetrating into a new world,' he wrote in his book *Half Mile Down*.

Beebe went down hundreds of times with his primitive open helmet resting on his shoulders. He began to think of constructing a cylinder to take him into the deep sea and met Otis Barton, an engineer who was already working along these lines. Together they produced the first bathysphere, a steel ball without joints, 3.88m (12ft 9in) in diameter, with walls 38mm ($1\frac{1}{2}$in) thick.

By 1934 they had arrived at a depth of 765m (2510ft) – the 'half mile' of the title to Beebe's book. There was always the risk of the cable snapping in a swell which would leave them forever at the bottom.

The descents in the bathysphere were very important because Beebe was a trained scientist and even today his observations are more important to the naturalist than those of some of his unqualified successors. He recorded the flashes made by unknown organisms in the deep sea and found many fishes previously unknown to science.

The Piccards and the Bathyscaphe

The first real craft designed for the exploration of the deep sea was produced by Professor Auguste Piccard from Switzerland. He had already constructed a successful balloon to explore the stratosphere and in 1938 he began to consider an underwater balloon. His 'bathyscaphe' (or deep ship) consisted of a steel observation chamber linked to a balloon filled with petrol which made it lighter than water.

The first bathyscaphe was financed by the Belgium National Scientific Research Fund known by its initials FNRS. The war interrupted the development work but soon afterwards the first bathyscaphe, FNRS 2 (the balloon had been FNRS 1) was launched. On 26 October 1948 she made her first successful dive off the Cape Verde Islands and an unmanned dive to 1380m (4527ft). Unfortunately the bathyscaphe was damaged by being towed in heavy seas and Piccard designed a new and stronger version. With the aid of the French Admiralty a new FRNS 3 was built at Toulon.

There was some difficulty between the Swiss physicist and the French Naval Engineers and then in 1951 Professor Piccard received an offer to build another bathyscaphe in Italy. He jumped at the chance. The Italian version was named *Trieste* and had a greater depth capability.

The *Trieste* was eventually bought by the US Navy for research. In 1957 26 dives were carried out in the Mediterranean and in 1958 the Navy equipped her with a new deep diving sphere. On the 23 January 1960 it achieved its final triumph. Piloted by Jacques Piccard and Lieutenant Donald Walsh of the US Navy it reached bottom in the deepest part of the ocean, the Challenger Deep, 10,900m (35,800ft) down off Guam in the Pacific. Piccard arrived there after nearly five hours of descending to find a small red shrimp and flat fish on the bottom. He had finally proved that life could exist in the greatest depth of the sea.

The Piccards also developed and built a drifting mid-water submersible, the Mesoscaphe, which took scientists on a drift dive along the Gulf Stream in 1969.

Research Diving

One main use of the aqualung has been in marine bottom studies of the rocky sub-littoral area. The apparatus provides the only sure way of sampling as trawls and dredgers can not work efficiently on the sandy bottom. Small animals can for the first time be observed in their natural habitat. The habitats themselves can be classified and studied and the animals can be collected in first class condition for museums and research collections.

Many marine animals were considered rare until divers and scientists swam freely to the sea bed using aqualungs. Such animals included the nudibranchs and such fish as the leopard spotted goby. Most British universities have special branches of the British Sub-Aqua Club where undergraduates can learn to dive for their studies or for pure enjoyment.

Fisheries research has been helped by the use of the aqualung to watch fishing gear being used underwater. The first photographs of trawls in operation were taken by Jimmy Hodges, the ex-Royal Navy frogman. Research into sea life in the Mediterranean has been carried out by Professor Riedl and others and many marine laboratories throughout the world use the aqualung every day for research.

In Britain the Field Studies Council organises marine biology courses for divers at their centres at Dale and Orielton in Pembrokeshire. Dr Keith Hiscock instructs in underwater research methods and techniques on the Island of Lundy in the Bristol Channel. Lundy has set up the first underwater nature reserve in the British Isles and many unusual species flourish there.

The principal universities in the United Kingdom providing the opportunity for marine research and diving are University College Swansea, Bangor University, Menai Bridge Marine Station, Liverpool University at Port Erin in the Isle of Man and Durham University in conjunction with Dr David Bellamy. There are well known marine research establishments at the Marine Biological Association

127

Headquarters at Plymouth and at the Scottish Marine Biological Association at Oban. In Great Britain much research is financed by the Natural Environment Research Council (NERC). The Nature Conservancy Council organises coastal surveys. In the USA the two most famous Marine Research Establishments that use diving are the Scripps Institution in California and the Woods Hole Station in Massachusetts. There are also marine laboratories in Bermuda and Jamaica that have extensive diving facilities.

In all these diving operations underwater photography provides a means of recording the undersea condition. Most diving scientists and those interested in the subject belong to the Underwater Association for Scientific Research which was founded in 1965. Its diving members include both professionals and amateurs and an annual symposium is held at the British Museum (Natural History). This covers the whole field of diving science. A newsletter is published regularly and the Association produces a code of practice for scientific diving.

The new science of underwater archaeology owes everything to the aqualung and a number of projects have already been described. George Bass of the University of Pennsylvania brought the science to a new level with his painstaking and accurate excavations in the Mediterranean. This high standard has been continued by Michael Katzev working in Cyprus. The use of the air lift to remove sand and mud from ancient wrecks has proved invaluable.

Many other disciplines have benefitted from aqualung diving, the notable underwater researchers in Britain include Professor Alan Baddely (nitrogen narcosis), Dr Helen Ross (orientation of divers), Dr Duncan Godden (psychology of divers) and Dr David Baume who has pioneered underwater engineering courses. In the United States Dr Glenn Egstrom and Dr Arthur Bachrach have worked together on the question of diver panic, diver's equipment and many other subjects.

Geologists may also use the aqualung to obtain rock samples and to observe sand movement. In up-welling 'hotpoints' in volcanic areas of the sea bed strange forms of animal life are to be found.

One of the best known underwater explorers and scientists is an unassuming Canadian Doctor of Medicine, Joe McInnes. He has run the first underwater living experiments under the ice in the Canadian Arctic and his films of whales such as *In Search of the Bow Head Whale* are breathtakingly exciting.

Many diving doctors belong to the Undersea Medical Society which was founded in 1967 in Washington. The society aims to help the advance of undersea medicine and supporting sciences. It assists communication between medical research workers and publishes a journal *Undersea Biomedical Research*, and a regular newsletter *Pressure*.

Police Divers

The aqualung is also a valuable tool for police forces involved with search and recovery of bodies or stolen articles. In Britain many police groups were originally taught by branches of the British Sub-Aqua Club. The club also provided divers for urgent searches when needed.

There are currently 29 police underwater search units in the country, each containing approximately 10 divers and supervised by an inspector or sergeant. Five of the teams are full time and there are police diving schools at Glasgow and in Northumbria. These run four week courses. Training is also carried out at home stations once per week.

The aqualung is normally used though occasionally surface demand equipment is needed. The police use full face masks and dry suits for their recovery operations.

Army Diving

The Royal Engineers, as already described, formed the first team of working divers in the early nineteenth century. They carry on the tradition today. Their course at Marchwood near Southampton is recognised by the Government to issue the official basic air-diving commercial certificate (see below).

After the days of Colonel Pasley, diving in the Royal Engineers was within 'Submarine Mining Companies' whose responsibilities included the defence of Navy dockyards, by laying mine fields offshore and general demolitions. However, in 1905 the Navy took over all these responsibilities and army diving virtually ceased. It began again during World War I and in World War 2 the Royal Engineers were still using helmets while working to keep ports operational. They supplied at least one of the crew of a successful midget submarine – Sgt Shaw DCM.

After World War 2 a Port Training Regiment was formed and by 1961 a cadre of Royal Engineers divers had been created. In 1965 the Royal Engineers Diving School was re-started under its present commander Lieutenant Colonel Peter Chitty MBE with the task of training 260 shallow water divers. The school became well established and by 1968 had trained hundreds of army divers. Each field squadron had a team of approximately a dozen divers equipped with

Modern Royal Navy divers use a commercial compressed air diving set which has been adapted for service use, and is very similar to conventional aqualungs.

Heinke aqualungs and compressors.

In the 1970s the Royal Engineers have been engaged in 'Engineering for Peace' – a programme to help developing countries with projects that range from reef reconnaissance on Caribbean Islands to building jetties in Cyprus. Their activities have included piling, concreting, cutting and welding, helping local police and exploring sewers!

The Royal Engineers use compressed air diving equipment only and there are three different sets. These are; the Aquarius, produced by Submarine Products, the Aga Divator and the Kirby Morgan Six.

The Army Compressed Air Diver (basic training) course lasts four weeks and gives the trainee twenty hours under water. The Army Advanced Diver course is eight weeks of underwater engineering and on successful completion the Training Services Agency Basic Air Diving Certificate is presented, thus providing the soldier with a valuable commercial qualification. Ranks above corporal may take a three week Army Diving Supervisor's course learning management and control of a team of divers.

In 1979 the army had approximately 330 Royal Engineer trained divers and 80 divers in other arms of the service all of whom had been trained at Marchwood. Diving in the army does not provide a full time career although engineering does. Recruits are first trained in basic engineering skills and are then selected after aptitude tests for diving.

There is also army diving in the United States with the US Corps of Engineers, and in some NATO countries such as the Netherlands, Belgium and West Germany.

Navy Diving
There are two types of divers in the Royal Navy, the part-time 'ship's' diver and the fully professional 'clearance' diver.

Ship's Divers
Each ship will have a ship's diver to deal with routine hull maintenance and searches down to a maximum depth of 30m (100ft). Some will also have a Ship's Diving Officer who plans and supervises this work and the team. A frigate will normally carry two SDOs and six SDs. There may also be a diving supervisor who is a senior ship's diver who has completed a further course.

Ship's divers originally used the Navy's own compressed air breathing set (SABA) but are now equipped with Aquarius self-contained apparatus which has two cylinders of compressed air and a

131

Clearance divers, the professionals of the Royal Navy, employ equipment using breathing mixtures of oxygen and nitrogen, or else pure oxygen equipment as illustrated.

face mask covering eyes, nose and mouth. The cylinders are charged to 170 kilos per square centimetre (2400 pounds per square inch).

Clearance Divers
These are now merely known as 'divers' in the service and are considered to be the only professionals in the Royal Navy.

Ratings qualify as Seamen Divers. These men can carry out searches of ships' bottoms and also other duties and operations down to a depth of 55m (180ft). They may use compressed air, mixtures, or pure oxygen. They are trained in rescue, first aid and mine disposal and operation of the Navy's inflatable Gemini dinghies. They use BASCA (Breathing Apparatus Self-Contained Compressed Air) or the Aquarius and CDBA (Clearance Diving Breathing Apparatus) which is also autonomous but is designed for mixture breathing. There are normally four mixtures of oxygen and nitrogen that are used, or pure oxygen.

Leading Divers qualify to use surface demand equipment and to act as attendants for deep diving down to 75m (246ft). They assist in explosive ordnance disposal operations and in compression chambers. They are also trained to deal with attacks by underwater saboteurs and in beach clearance and reconnaisance.

Petty Officer Divers plan and supervise all diving operations and instruct the techniques of diving demolition and explosive disposal. They deal with the training of divers at sea and administrate the clearance diving teams.

Mine Warfare and Clearance Diving Officers will have completed a seven month course consisting of fourteen weeks diving, seven weeks of ordnance disposal and eleven weeks of mine warfare. He will normally be assigned to a minesweeper.

Diving Training
The headquarters of diving training is at the Navy Submarine base at HMS *Vernon* in Portsmouth Harbour. A ship's diver training course is four weeks and the division has two fleet tenders for the use of career courses. Both vessels carry recompression chambers.

Clearance Diving Teams
There are seven special teams for advanced operations.

Such diving teams are called on in an emergency to recover aircraft that crash into the sea and with saturation systems they have a capability down to 330m (1000ft). Teams were used to clear the Suez Canal following the hostilities between Egypt and Israel.

In 1977 Lieutenant Commander David Bartlett led a team of Royal Navy divers to work in co-operation with the Egyptian Navy to rescue the temple of Augustus Caesar dating from 12 B.C. from the waters of Aswan. The temple had been underwater since the building of the low dam of Aswan in 1902 and the intention was to raise the temple and to reconstruct it alongside other monuments. Before the temple blocks, many weighing more than a tonne, could be located, reached, marked, attached by hawsers to air bags and lifted to the surface, 2000 tonnes of mud had to be cleared. This was done with water jets and air lifts in zero visibility. All 320 blocks of the temple were raised and the operation was completed on schedule.

Another Royal Navy Diving Officer, Lieutenant Commander Thompson, helped the Egyptians to recover the Gate of Diocletian.

In 1980 the Royal Navy commissioned a new diving ship, the 7200 tonne *Challenger*. She is equipped to support divers operating down to 300m (1000ft) and as a mother ship for submersibles.

Careers

The Royal Navy provides diving careers and ratings complete their basic seamanship training at HMS *Raleigh* and then may be selected by an aptitude test for diving. There are training areas at Portsmouth, Portland, Falmouth and Oban. The Royal Navy submarine base at HMS *Dolphin* teaches submarine escape in a unique 30m (100ft) training tank and special suits have been developed for this purpose.

The Royal Marines also continue their diving tradition using oxygen sets.

5
Commercial Diving

Development
The conventional closed helmet diving dress described in Chapter 1 continued until recently to be the standard equipment for working underwater. Siebe Gorman Ltd continued to flourish after Siebe's death in 1872 carried on by his sons and son-in-law. Robert Davis took over as Managing Director towards the end of the nineteenth century, working on many new developments. Versions of the original closed helmet dress were made in many parts of the world and each industrialised country developed its own variants.

Traditional Helmet Diving
The traditional way of supplying air to these 'hard hat' divers was by way of hand pumps, although compressors and air banks have been increasingly used during recent years. Each diver has a tender who is in touch with him through his 'life line' and also normally by telephone. Gauges on the pump at the surface show the diver's depth and the air pressure delivered. The diving suit is made of sheet rubber between two layers of tanned twill and watertight joints are made at the neck and wrists. The suit is clamped by studs to a 'corselet' or metal breastplate on the diver's chest and the helmet in turn screws into this. Besides a weight belt and lead soled shoes, the diver carries front and back weights on the corselet, the whole weighing approximately 85kg (187lb).

The helmets and corselets are made of tinned copper with brass attachments. In the front of the helmet is the 'front glass' through which he sees. At the sides are two more glasses protected by guards.

The conventional helmet diving system was enormously successful and was used in hundreds of underwater salvage operations during the nineteenth century. Many modern lightweight helmets are built on much the same principles. Perhaps the best known and most successful salvage operators were the firm of Cox and Danks who 'bought a navy' – the wrecks of the German Fleet scuttled in Scapa Flow in World War 1.

Robert Davis went on to develop the Davis Submarine Escape

apparatus and many other kinds of equipment. He was knighted in 1932, soon after the first sailors had escaped from the Royal Navy submarine *Poseidon* wearing his light weight apparatus. His book, *Deep Diving and Submarine Operations*, became a classic textbook and also a highly readable account of divers' exploits. During World War 2 the Admiralty Experimental Diving Unit under Commander Bill Shelford was housed in the works of Siebe Gorman at Chessington and experimental work was carried on developing special military diving systems.

'SCUBA' and Hookah Gear

The marketing of the aqualung or SCUBA after World War 2 introduced a second very successful commercial diving system and it was soon used on such operations as the inspection of pipes on the seabed and the cleaning and underwater painting of ships. The conventional helmet diver standing in his lead boots and completely protected from the elements had the edge on his more manoeuverable colleague when it came to hard work on the bottom but the aqualung could also be adapted with a pipe to the surface. Another form of lightweight apparatus is known as 'hookah' or 'surface demand' gear. Air is pumped down and passes through a conventional aqualung demand valve to the diver. He can put on extra weight so that he can be anchored firmly on the bottom for working and can then change his fins for shoes.

In the twenty years between 1945 and 1965 commercial interest in deep diving was limited to the occasional salvage operation. Commercial diving was mainly concerned with dock and harbour work usually in depths of about 10m (30ft). During the late 1950s and early 1960s the enormous potential of the underwater gas fields became apparent and in 1965 British Petroleum first struck gas in the North Sea. It became clear that sooner or later divers would have to go deeper and stay longer.

Gas Mixtures

In 1955 Sir Robert Davis had produced a number of specifications for underwater houses in which divers might stay for several days. The first problem in deep diving lay with the gas mixtures that were breathed. Compressed air, the most natural and easily obtainable mixture was successfully used by helmet and aqualung divers. However, there was the ever present problem of bends and, even more important, the increasing effect of nitrogen narcosis at depth. It was generally felt that 40m (130ft) was a good maximum for sports

136

divers. Experienced instructors and professionals operated successfully at 60m (200ft) but below this the risks rapidly increased and
efficiency dropped. Eventually the commercial diving regulations
fixed the limit at 50m (164ft). This depth capability was not enough to
service the new oilfield developments.

The nitrogen in the air seemed to cause most of the problems and
experiments were made using other breathing mixtures which sub-
stituted other gases for this troublesome ingredient. in 1945 Arne
Zetterstrom, a 28 year old Swedish engineer had completed a successful dive to 110m (363ft) in the Baltic breathing a mixture of oxygen
and hydrogen. On his next dive he reached an incredible 161m (528ft)
safely but was killed when his tenders made an inexcusable mistake
and pulled him rapidly to the surface. Although this was a break-
through the change-over at depth from compressed air to oxy-
hydrogen was not simple and it is a potentially explosive mixture.
Zetterstrom's experiments were not continued but led to the specu-
lation that one day man might be adapted to breathe another mixture
of hydrogen and oxygen – water!.

Helium
In 1919 Professor Elihu Thomson in Massachusetts had suggested the
use of helium in place of nitrogen for deep diving. It was tried out in
1925 and seemed to cut decompression times by a quarter. It also
allowed the divers to remain clear-headed at depth, eliminating
nitrogen narcosis. In the 1930s further experiments were run in
Britain by the Admiralty and Siebe Gorman Ltd and in the USA by
Drs Behnke and Yarborough who successfully compressed a diver to
150m (500ft) in a tank.

In 1936 a young graduate of the Massachusetts Instute of
Technology, Max Nohl, had developed a new type of helmet with a
circular glass plate giving 360° vision and which could be linked to
cylinders to be self-contained. This proved an ideal vehicle for
mixture breathing and Nohl contacted a friend, Dr Edgar End,
suggesting that they try out the helium mixtures. Dr End produced a
decompression schedule for helium and the first experimental dive
took place in the recompression chamber at Milwaukee Hospital. Nohl
and his co-worker, Craig, breathed a mixture of 79% helium and 21%
oxygen for an hour. The experiment was a complete success.

The Americans were lucky to have the only easily available natural
supplies of helium in the world. The mixture that would allow man to
dive down to the limits of the continental shelf was now ready but
there still remained the problem of decompression. Although times

137

were less on helium they were still too long for efficient diving.

A notable example was the salvage of the United States submarine, *Squalus* in 1939. She had sunk to a depth of 74m (243ft). US Navy divers attached a rescue chamber to the submarine's hatch and in four trips brought 33 crew members safely back to the surface. The divers made over 600 dives using helium but because of the time needed for decompression they could work for only 10 minutes on the bottom each time they dived.

In 1948 Captain 'Bill' Shelford commanded the Royal Navy's diving ship, *Reclaim*. Using some of the last helium supplies left in Britain he organised a set of deep helium dives in Loch Fyne. These culminated in Petty Officer Wilfred Bollard successfully breaking the world depth record with a dive in a conventional helmet to 165m (540ft). His successful decompression schedule took $8\frac{1}{2}$ hours. Lieutenant George Wookey, Royal Navy, broke the record again descending to 183m (600ft) in 1954.

Hannes Keller

1939 had seen the beginning of World War 2 and an end to these experiments as divers and scientists were given other duties.

After the war scientists again began to consider the problems. In 1962 a young mathematician with little knowledge of diving, who came from a country with no coastline or diving history, calmly announced that he had developed a secret mixture which would allow him to go to a depth of 305m (1000ft), stay 5 minutes, and return to the surface in $4\frac{1}{2}$ hours. Few scientists had believed the story of the young Hannes Keller from Winterthur in Switzerland until, in a series of solo and hair-raising experiments, he successfully reached a depth of 229m (750ft) returning in only 34 minutes! Experts such as Dr 'Val' Hempleman of the Royal Navy Physiological Laboratory and Dr George Bond of the US Navy were now extremely interested.

The US Navy gave Keller the back-up for his 305m (1000ft) experiment. He was to descend in a bell with Peter Small, the journalist who had co-founded the British Sub-Aqua Club. Two experienced stand-by divers, Chris Whittaker from Britain and Richard Anderson from the United States, would be ready to help while the bell was within diving range. At a depth of 305m (1000ft) Keller would open the hatch and make a brief foray to plant the Swiss flag ceremonially on the bottom. Many pressures built up but Keller decided not to postpone the dive when he discovered that one of his four storage tanks of mixture was only at half pressure.

All went according to plan until Keller left the bell. He became

The first experimental dive to over 300m ended in tragedy. Hannes Keller (lower right), whose fin became caught in the bell's hatch, survived but his companion Peter Small (upper right) died.

entangled in the flag which proved to be ridiculously large. A desperate two minute struggle ensued. Keller returned with only seconds left before unconsciousness. The end of his fin became stuck in the hatch when he closed it and caused yet more problems. Keller managed to order the return of the bell. At 61m (200ft) the bell was stopped and Whittaker and Anderson dived to cut the fin free. They lost contact and only Anderson came back. When the bell was finally opened Keller was alive but Small was dead. Keller had proved his theory but not the safety of his method. The record was to stand for many years.

Saturation Diving Theory
Research began to show that when a diver spent very long periods on the bottom he eventually reached the stage where his body was fully 'saturated' with gas and could absorb no more. His decompression was then the same no matter how long he stayed. The concept of saturation diving was thus born. Men could live under the sea – possibly for months at a time – and still return to the surface, albeit slowly, decompressing for maximum exposure. During the 1960s and early 1970s therefore a number of experiments in underwater living were undertaken by various groups and individuals.

Undersea Living
In the years immediately preceeding Hannes Keller's astonishing dive Cousteau had been preparing to put his first 'aquanauts' on the sea bed, realising the importance that the technique might have for future oilfield developments. At the same time Edwin Link, an American millionaire and inventor of the war-time 'Link trainer' for pilots, became interested in undersea living and built his own underwater house in which a solo Belgian diver, Robert Stenuit, spent 24 hours on the first of his 'Man in the Sea' projects. The US Navy too were making massive preparations for their own foray down to the continental shelf known more scientifically as *Sealab*.

Link and Cousteau both launched their first experiments in 1962, that of Link pre-dating Cousteau's by only a few days. Both were completely successful. They both organised a further experiment before the first of the Sealabs was launched off Bermuda. By this time Link had successfully maintained Stenuit at a depth of 132m (432ft) for 49 hours and Cousteau's aquanauts, more interested in time than depth, had lived underwater for 30 days.

In 1965 the first amateur full-scale underwater living experiment was mounted by Bournemouth branch of the BSAC. A steel house called *Glaucus* 3.66m (12ft) long by 2.14m (7ft) in diameter was placed 9.15m (30ft) down in Plymouth Sound. Two enterprising members, 19-year-old Colin Irwin and 21-year-old John Heath lived successfully inside for a week. They survived a force 11 gale and proved that amateur divers could contribute even in this specialised field. Glaucus is now owned by the Fort Bovisand Underwater Centre and divers still visit it on the bottom in Plymouth Sound.

The driving force behind the United States Navy programme was the 'father of saturation diving', Captain George Bond. As a doctor he had been active in diving medicine for many years. His *Sealab I* experiment was cut short by an impending hurricane but it was a major success.

Sealab II was a much larger operation in which three teams of ten men took it in turns to spend ten days on the bottom. Astronaut Commander Scott Carpenter was a member of one of the teams and spoke from the habitat by radio to astronaut Gordon Cooper whose space craft *Gemini* was circling the earth 330km (220 miles) above and also to Cousteau in his *Conshelf III* experiment under 100m (328ft) of water off Nice. History had been made. Man had dared greatly and survived.

The US Navy generously invited the Royal Navy, the Royal Canadian Navy and the Royal Australian Navy to send experienced divers to take part in *Sealab III* and Lt Cmdr Cyril Rafferty and Petty Officer Mike Clark RN did so. The experiment struck trouble when approaching the 183m (600ft) level. Although many simulated dives using the mixture 98% helium, and 2% oxygen had taken place it was found that the aquanauts suffered extremely from cold when in the sea and Berry Cannon, one of *Sealab III*'s crew became unconscious while trying to open a hatch. He was dragged back to the habitat by his companion diver but was already dead. *Sealab III* was ended on this sombre note.

1969 saw the first undersea living and working by scientists in the United States. They worked at comparatively shallow depths in the *Tektite* house (tektites are small glassy pieces of mineral found in the sea and on land and believed to have come from outer space) off the United States Virgin Islands. One team, led by Dr Sylvia Earl, was composed entirely of women researchers. Dr Brian Ray of the UK built an inflatable shallow habitat off Malta which operated successfully and very cheaply.

Undersea living in the shallower depths had become almost commonplace and just another tool of the professional scientist.

Table 2 lists some of the underwater living experiments.

Table 2 UNDERWATER LIVING EXPERIMENTS

Year	Project	Organised by	Site	Depth	Duration	Habitat	Number of Aquanauts	Name of Aquanauts	Mixture
1962	Man in the Sea I	Ed Link (USA)	Villefranche Mediterranean	60m (200ft)	24 hrs	Cylinder 3m × 1m (10ft × 3ft)	1	Robert Stenuit	3% O_2 97% He
1962	Comshelf I (PreContinent I)	Jacques Cousteau (France)	Marseille Mediterranean	10m (33ft)	7 days	Cylinder 5.2m × 2.4m (17ft × 8ft)	2	Falco & Wesley	Air & HeO
1963	Comshelf II (PreContinent II)	Jacques Cousteau (France)	Shaab-Rumi Red Sea	11m (36ft)	30 days	Starfish House 10m (34ft) at widest point	5	Falco, Wesley, Servalo and others	Air
				27m (90ft)	7 days	Deep cabin vertical cylinder 2.3m × 4.9m (7½ft × 16ft)	2		5% O_2 20% N_2 75% He
1964	Man in the Sea II (SPID)	Ed Link (USA)	Great Stirrup Cay Bahamas	132m (432ft)	49 hrs	2m × 1.06m (6ft-6in × 3ft-6in) submarine portable inflatable dwelling	2	Stenuit and Lindbergh	4% O_2 96% He
1964	Sealab I	US Navy (Capt G Bond)	Argus Is. Bermuda	59m (193ft)	11 days	Cylinder 12m × 2.75m (40ft × 9ft)	4	Barth, Manning Anderson, Dr Anderson	4% O_2 17% N_2 79% He
1965	Comshelf III	Jacques Cousteau (France)	French Mediterranean	100m (330ft)	22 days	Sphere 5.5m (18ft) diameter 13.7m (45ft) long	6	Laban, Rollet Philippe Cousteau J-C Dumas, Barpiarelli	1.9–2.3% O_2 1% H_2 bal He
1965	Glaucus	Bourmouth Branch – BSAC	Plymouth England	9m (30ft)	7 days	Cylinder 3.7m × 2.1m (12ft × 7ft)	2	Colin Irwen & John Heath	Air
1965	Sealab II	US Navy (Capt G Bond)	La Jolla California	63m (205ft)	10 days	Cylinder 3.7m × 17.4m (12ft × 57ft)	3 teams of 10 men each	including Cdr Scott Carpenter	4% O_2

Year	Project	Organised by	Site	Depth	Duration	Habitat	Number of Aquanauts	Name of Aquanauts	Mixture
1966	Hydrolab	Unexo (USA)	Freeport Bahamas	12m (39ft)		Cylinder 4.5m × 2.4m (15ft × 8ft)	Various	Continuous occupation 1970–77	Air
1969	Sealab III	US Navy (Capt G Bond)	California	180m (600ft)	13 days (suspended)	Cylinder 18m (60ft) long housing 9 men at a time	45 divers 5 teams of 9 men	including Cdr Scott Carpenter (Astronaut)	92% He 2% O_2 6% N_2
1969	SDM IQ 1 & 2	Dr B Ray (UK)	Malta Mediterranean	6m (20ft)	10 man days	Inflatable habitats	1–2	—	Air
1969	Heligoland Laboratory	West Germany	Heligoland N. Sea	20m (65ft)	10 days	9m × 6m × 3m (30ft × 20ft × 10ft)	8 men	Numerous occupations	Air
1969	Tektite I	US Multi-Agency	Lameshur Bay US Virgin Islands	15m (50ft)	60 days	2 vertical cylinders 5.5m × 3.8m (18ft × 12½ft) joined by tunnel	4		NO_2
1970	Makai Range	US Navy	Hawaii	158m (520ft)	5 days	15m × 4.5m (50ft × 15ft)	6		
1970	Tektite II	US Multi-Agency	Virgin Islands	15m (50ft)	12–30 days each team	2 vertical cylinders 5.5m × 3.8m (18ft × 12½ft) joined by tunnel	11 teams of 5 divers each	included one team of female scientists let by Dr Sylvia Earle	
1971/2	Makai Range	US Navy	Hawaii	24m 61m (80ft 200ft)	Bounce 10 days	15m × 4.5m (50ft × 15ft)	6		

Experiments have also been carried out in the USSR, Cuba, Bulgaria, Czechoslovakia, the Netherlands, Poland, Italy and Rumania.

143

Simulated dives in pressure chambers demonstrated the problems of very deep diving. In 1970 John Bevan of the Royal Navy Physiological Laboratory was one of the first to work successfully at over 450m.

Simulated Dives

Careful preparation was obviously needed in going deeper and a number of simulated dives took place in the years immediately following *Sealab III* and *Tektite*.

They were organised in pressurised chambers where the volunteers worked and lived in a mixed gas atmosphere and at high pressures equivalent to the greater depths of the continental shelf. These 'hyperbaric' chambers existed at navy research establishments and already the larger diving contractors concerned with the fast developing area of the North Sea were building their own. The chambers also included wet 'pots' where the researchers could do experiments in water while under pressure.

Swiss researchers in a simulated dive at Alverstoke in England had suffered from a new phenomenon at a depth of approximately 300m (1000ft). This produced trembling of the fingers and other physiological symptoms. It became known as HPNS (High Pressure Nervous

Syndrome). In 1970 two scientists, John Bevan and Peter Sharphouse, working for the Royal Navy, successfully passed this barrier, spending ten hours at a simulated depth of 458m (1500ft). They were both active amateur divers and members of the British Sub-Aqua Club, illustrating the close links that exist between the three types of diving – amateur, scientific and military. This simulated dive was under the direction of Dr Peter Bennett now at Duke University in the USA. He tried a new method of mixing gases known as 'Tri-mix' which overcame the HPNS problem. Soon afterwards the French diving company, Comex, successfully pressurised two men to a simulated 520m (1700ft) at Marseille. Later they went to 610m (2000ft) the divers spending 24 days decompressing for the six hours spent at this depth. In 1980 Peter Bennet successfully took three volunteers to a simulated depth of 650m (2132ft) in a pressure tank at Duke. They suffered no ill effects and worked safely at this new world record depth.

These experiments charted the way ahead but every day of the year commercial divers were routinely working in harbours, dams and far out to sea. They were already beginning to go much deeper.

Modern Commercial Diving

Everyday commercial diving is not, of course, an end in itself, but a means of getting to a job. Most divers are concerned with the mundane tasks of inspection, construction, maintenance or demolition. The field can be conveniently divided into two areas – air diving and deep or mixed gas diving. Each of these has its own techniques, problems and even its own type of divers.

Air Diving

Civil engineering divers mainly use air as their breathing mixture and under existing British regulations can operate down to a maximum depth of 50m (165ft). They are thus the direct descendants of the nineteenth century helmet divers carrying out much of the same work using more modern techniques. What sort of tasks do they carry out?

A variety of inspections are necessary whenever man builds structures in the sea. Divers will check on the stability of the sea bottom, on lock gates and inlet valves and many other features. This work was sometimes carried out using SCUBA (as the aqualung is usually known in commercial circles). However the 'Kirby Morgan' band mask system has the advantage that the supervisor on the surface can speak directly to the working diver and get 'blow by blow' reports of the progress. In polluted waters divers will use lightweight helmets which completely protect them from contact with the water. The diver will often take an underwater camera to make an accurate record of the situation on the bottom.

Often these divers are working in harbours and other places where the underwater visibility is zero. When the water is so 'black' that he cannot see his depth gauge the diver must be controlled from the surface. The depth will be checked before the dive and the time on the bottom carefully monitored from the surface. Even in very low visibility conditions intensified light television cameras may be used giving a better view than the naked eye.

Many 'small' tasks are carried out by air divers. These include repairing masonry, cutting sheet piling and removing obstructions. Frequently stolen vehicles that have been dumped have to be investigated and recovered for the police. Repairs range from collapsed or collapsing bridges to jammed valves and rotting brick work.

Divers regularly check the banks of rivers such as the Thames, clearing debris and brick work and filling in holes. This type of work will probably be carried out from a barge and water jets will be used for cleaning.

Underwater structures often have to be tested to check on corrosion and deterioration. This technique is known as NDT (Non-Destructive Testing). Ultra-Sonic methods can also be used.

The larger jobs may include clearing rocks and blasting and excavating. High pressure hydro-jetting is widely used.

It may be necessary to demolish a ship completely if it is proving a hazard and to level it to the sea bed.

The Thames Barrier
Perhaps the largest civil engineering diving operation in the world is the Thames Barrier project which is designed to ensure that London will be protected from disastrous flooding in the event of extra high tides coinciding with fresh weather blowing up the estuary. London is slowly sinking and tide levels have risen by 60cm (2ft) at London Bridge over the last 100 years. A freak flood could be catastrophic, flooding the underground system and causing an estimated thousand million pounds' worth of damage.

The barrier, when completed, will stretch all the way across the Woolwich Reach. It consists of a series of huge steel gates between great concrete islands. The first step in building the islands was to drive interlocking steel piles 15m (50ft) into the bed of the Thames. The sub-contractors are Shiers Diving Contracts Limited, started by

Don Shiers, director of the diving sub-contrators involved in the building of the huge Thames Barrier project, photographed against the scene of his operations.

Don Shiers one of the first training officers of the London Branch of the BSAC and an ex-Royal Marine diver. Shiers had to design wedges to prevent the river caving in these hollow dams before they were filled with concrete. His divers had positioned the huge joists in up to 25m (80ft) of muddy, icy water. The Shiers solution to the wedging was to blow up plastic bags with concrete through a pipe from the surface. It worked and the divers carried on to blast away the floor of the dam to make a flat, solid base for 18m (60ft) of reinforced concrete which was needed to withstand the enormous pressure of the Thames in full flood.

Qualities of Divers
What does it take to be a successful diver under the these conditions? Shiers rates enthusiasm as the most important quality – the diver should not be in the business just for the money. 98% of his divers began as sports divers and built up their interest from there, stimulated by love of diving and the chance of a reasonable reward for their ability. They have to be strong and fit and previous

147

experience at cutting or welding is a distinct advantage. Training at one of the government recognised schools is a good beginning but needs to be followed by real 'on the job' experience.

Is this form of commercial diving as dangerous as it seems to the layman? It need not be so, providing the diver really understands the laws of diving physiology. Such knowledge is gained during sports diver training and divers with this background are used to having to think for themselves. Regular medical examinations are compulsory. One of the most unpleasant and taxing jobs carried out by Shiers' divers involved cutting piping in 2.4m (8ft) diameter shaft at a depth of 50m (160ft). It was unpleasant because the shaft was full of bentonite, not water. The white sludge is used in sewage schemes. The diver involved worked in nil visibility.

Breathing Apparatus
Much of modern civil engineering diving is carried out using full face masks or light-weight helmets which can combine some of the best features of traditional helmet and SCUBA gear. Voice communication is very important.

The Kirby Morgan band mask is rather similar to a full face mask that was originally developed for amateur divers by the Normalair Company. It is very widely used with an airline or with cylinders on the diver's back. Other full face masks such as the Avon and Aga are also used. Their function is to provide the professional diver with a comfortable well-fitting mask that will protect him from cold and give good communication with the surface and a wide field of vision. Breathing is through a small oral-nasal mask within. They are generally more economical on the breathing mixture than the light-weight helmet.

The 'Swindell' helmet is a fibre glass helmet provided with a neck seal and is fixed to the diver by a body belt. 'Divex' and 'Aquadyne' helmets are widely used. The helmets have the advantage of comfort and free-flow air or mixture but cannot be used if the amount of breathing mixture is limited. The 'standard' helmet dress is still used very occasionally, its advantage being that it has air space all round the body in very cold and very murky conditions.

Self-contained SCUBA has been used for simple inspections although the diver seldom uses fins in low visibility. In these conditions it is often better to know at least one positive direction i.e. 'down' by being heavily weighted and having one's feet planted firmly on the bottom. Cages are used whenever possible so that supervisors on the surface know that the diver is at the right depth and in position.

Tasks

The traditional tasks of the shallow water diver were cutting and welding but divers now have to use hydraulic and air tools and know how to use survey cameras and explosives.

Three main types of cutting apparatus are available – oxy-hydrogen cutters, oxy-arc system and thermic lances. Oxy-acetylene, a normal method above the surface, cannot be used deep underwater and so hydrogen and oxygen are supplied (through separate hoses). The combination of the gases generates enough heat to melt steel once the heat is concentrated.

The oxy-arc type of equipment is used when a power supply is available and avoids the need to carry supplies of hydrogen to the site. The oxygen is supplied to an arc rod of carbon or steel and no air should be used. The oxy-arc method is generally considered the best as the surface to be cut needs little preparation.

When it is necessary to cut steel or even concrete rapidly a thermic lance can be used. This involves high pressure oxygen being fed through a tube packed with steel and magnesium rods. When the end is heated the steel burns fiercely, providing an enormous amount of heat.

Welding is a method of joining two metals together using a cleaning material known as a 'flux'. It is carried out with a coated rod, using the flux and a proofing material with an electric current passed through the centre. Really acceptable welds can only be made 'in the dry' and so this is often done inside a habitat on the bottom.

Welding is a complex process, a technique and also an art.

High pressure water jets are used for several underwater jobs. By varying the size of the jet different combinations of volume and pressure can be obtained. With a lower pressure and a higher volume they can be used for dispersing mud and sand, cleaning apparatus and burying pipes and cables. Using a higher pressure and a lower volume they are more useful for intensive cleaning and removing clinging material. In this form they can actually cut through sand-stone and even concrete. Water jets have been used to cut timber, piles and holes for explosive charges and, of course, for cleaning the hulls of ships.

Explosives are widely used in commercial diving for dispersing rock and wreck and for cutting channels and excavations. There are a number of types designed for specific tasks. Explosives are just another tool to be used by the diver.

Cartridge fired bolt guns are used for positioning plates and repairing piles. The Cox gun, developed by Cox and Danks of Scapa Flow fame, can fire bolts into 4cm ($1\frac{1}{2}$in) steel, using gunpowder which is stored in the head of each bolt. The barrel of the pistol-like gun is merely placed against the metal and the trigger pulled. A firing pin then activates the gunpowder which drives the bolt home. Cox guns have been used to fire air lines into sunken submarines to keep the trapped crew alive.

Cameras are part of the equipment of all modern commercial divers. They are used to check the type of sea floor, to investigate the problems encountered or to record work that has been completed. In low visibility, solicon-intensified cameras are used. These suffer less from reflection of particles in the water and in fact see better underwater than the diver can.

Offshore and Saturation Diving with Mixed Gases

The newest and most publicised form of commercial diving is that carried out from offshore oil rigs. It is also the deepest. These offshore divers are paid more than their civil engineering colleagues but have to put up with long periods on isolated rigs in generally unpleasant conditions. There is also a higher risk inseparable from diving in such areas as the north of the North Sea in winter.

Diving deaths inevitably attract publicity and it is in the interests of all concerned to keep these down to the absolute minimum. Britain's Department of Energy has a diving inspectorate led by Commander 'Jackie' Warner. They regulate activities and investigate all commercial diving accidents and make recommendations and rules for improvements to prevent them wherever possible.

Undersea Oilfields

The development of undersea oilfields is of immense importance to the nations who are lucky enough to have oil and gas deposits off their coasts and prospecting is continually going on. There are four main phases in the development of such an oilfield.

Firstly there is the 'acoustic' phase in which the rocks of the sea floor are examined to test whether or not they contain the structures that may hold deposits of oil or gas. This phase does not involve divers.

The second phase involves trial drilling of holes. In this 'exploration' phase divers begin to be involved. The drilling apparatus is designed to 'fail safe' but there are occasions when something goes wrong and then divers are sent down. Their activity here has been described as '50% a fire service and 50% an insurance policy'.

The third or 'construction' phase involves the location of production platforms and divers are involved every day in the business of connecting well heads and pipelines to shore. The pipe section may be 92cm (36in) in diameter and weigh many tonnes. Diving provides the means of getting an expert cutter or welder to the deep sea floor.

During this phase divers will also be engaged in repairing the rig and the pipelines and joining them together. Hyperbaric welding takes place 'in the dry' inside habitats which contain suitable breathing mixtures kept at the surrounding water pressure. Once the platform is operational, there will be a lot of inspection of pipelines and structures to be done. These involve the use of video and still cameras and various non-destructive testing techniques such as magnetic particle inspection or ultrasonics. Some of the inspection can be done using submersibles or remote controlled vehicles (RCVs) together with closed circuit television. These devices are constantly being improved, but will probably never entirely replace the diver.

The final stage in developing an oilfield is the 'production' phase. The platforms are usually semi-submersible with a catamaran hull and sit like vast tables in the sea. The drilling operations are situated near the centre of the rig and the oil and gas is collected and piped ashore or to waiting tankers.

The first offshore oilfields were developed in the 1960s and most of them are now concentrated in the North Sea. Drilling began in the southern North Sea and has moved northwards ever since.

Diving Techniques
The regulations in force in the United Kingdom require that all diving below 50m (165ft) should be done using a closed diving bell method. The present limit of diving is around 370m (1200ft) and several working dives have been succesfully carried out deeper than 300m (1000ft). The Comex diving company have carried out an experimental sea dive *Janus VIII* to 460m (1500ft). Diving services are provided by such diving contractors and those providing services to the oil companies offshore need considerable financial reserves as the cost of the bells and advanced equipment is high and the cost of paying and insuring their divers can be even higher.

There is a relatively small number of specialised deep diving contractors. Perhaps the largest of these are the American Taylor Diving and the Anglo-French Comex, followed closely by Oceaneering, Solus Ocean Systems, Sub Sea International, KD Marine, Seaway Diving, Thalassa Diving and 2W.

There are two main types of bell diving – 'bounce' dives and 'saturation' dives.

The bounce dive may be needed to correct or investigate some malfunction in the drilling equipment. This could mean diving as often as ten times in two days or only once in two months.

When an emergency occurs the diver will quite likely be roused from his bed at an unearthly hour with cold grey waves battering the rig. He and his companion will dress and go into the diving bell closing the hatch behind them. The steel bell will be lowered down a guide wire connected to the sea bed and as it submerges the water pressure seals the lower hatch, keeping atmospheric pressure inside.

When they arrive at the bottom which may be typically at 150 to 180m (500 to 600ft) they look through the port of the bell to assess the problem. Only after this do they need to pressurise the bell until their oxy-helium mixture (at depth often as little as 4% oxygen to 96% helium) is at the same pressure as the water outside. The lower hatch then falls open and the divers will go out helped by the 'bell man' and taking the necessary tools. This operation is known as a 'deep lockout'. The divers will be wearing a dry or water-heated suit and lightweight helmet or band mask. (The major companies have their own designs. Oceaneering's lightweight helmet is called the Rat Hat and Comex use their own 'Pro' band mask.) When leaving the bell the divers will be provided with an 'umbilical' which carries their breathing gas, power or hot water for suit heating and their communication cable. The dive may last 60–90 minutes during which the bell man will check the gas supply and tend the umbilicals. If there are no complications the diver will soon return to the bell, close the hatch and tell the 'topside' crew to start lifting.

Decompression from shallow depths may start inside the bell, being controlled by the divers. The bell will be hauled from the sea and swung aboard the rig where it is connected to a large deck pressure chamber. When the pressure inside the bell is equivalent to a depth of around 90m (300ft) they will transfer to the deck chamber which has previously been pressurised to this level. They can then decompress in relative comfort, have a meal, rest and read. A dive to 155m (510ft) for 30 minutes is likely to involve over 24 hours of decompression, so boredom can be a real problem.

In saturation diving, the divers live under pressure close to that of the seabed, on the surface to begin with. They then transfer under pressure (TUP) to their bell on the surface and descend direct to the seabed to work. The operation is somewhat similar to that of astronauts who transfer through a tunnel for moon walks. Saturation diving usually involves six to eight divers in a chamber with a schedule covering 24 hours.

Saturation divers at the surface will be kept at a pressure slightly less than the sea bed. They are lowered onto the bottom with the bell at this pressure and on arrival more oxy-helium is pumped in until the pressure is the same and a door at the bottom of the bell can be opened inwards. The divers can then lower themselves out until they see the bottom and position themselves if they need to leave the bell. A full band mask is usually worn and their diving equipment includes an 'on-off' tap for the mixture they use outside the bell and a harness so that they can be hauled back to the bell if necessary using a block and tackle.

During a saturation dive the divers will be under pressure for up to a month. Although the decompression takes so much longer than that for a bounce dive it is usually more incident free.

Surface Hyperbaric Complex
Most deep diving systems are now designed for saturation techniques to be used. At first surface chambers were of small diameter and the divers could not stand upright. Modern surface chambers have a diameter of up to about 2.4m (8ft) and usually there are two or three of them linked together by a large vertical storage chamber. This system allows several divers to be kept at different pressures for different dives. The bell, which is attached to the complex until needed, weighs over 3 tonnes and is let down by large winches through a hole in the rig deck known as the 'moon pool'. Although modern diving bells have a lock out capability they are mainly used for observation and have large viewing ports and external mechanical arms. They are capable of depths of 920m (3000ft) and make it possible for divers to work on the bottom for 18 hours out of 24 by using two or three crews in shifts.

'Jim'
Decompression is still a lengthy business. In Chapter 1 we outlined the development of armoured suits. The enormous advantage was that the body was still kept at atmospheric pressure inside and so could work for long periods exactly as on land without needing any decompression at all. As man penetrated deeper, however, the problem of getting the articulated joints to move seemed to be insuperable. Development ceased before World War 2 and did not start again until 1968 when a British company, Underwater and Marine Equipment Limited, already interested in reviving articulated or 'armoured'

153

diving suits, met, through a series of coincidences, the elderly Joseph Peress who had developed his armoured suit just after World War 1. The meeting between Mike Borrow and Mike Humphrey of UMEL resulted in one of the success stories of British Industry – *Jim* – named in honour of Jim Jarrett. DHB Construction Limited was formed to operate the new generation armoured suit and the first two suits *Jim* 2 and 3, which are still operational, have a depth capability of 300m (1000ft). *Jim* 2 has a cast magnesium alloy body, with a hinged dome with four acrylic view ports. The new articulted joints are machined from aluminium alloy and filled with a vegetable based oil. The life support system is very much like an astronaut's system, two external back mounted cylinders supply oxygen to replenish that used by the diver who wears an oro-nasal mask, his exhaled breath passing through a scrubber which absorbs the CO_2. *Jim* is 1.98m (6ft 6in) in height and weighs 360kg (800lb) on the surface with an operator inside. The apparatus can be lowered 300m (1000ft) in 5 minutes and the suit is flexible enough, weighing only 22kg (50lb) underwater, to walk up 45° ladders, roll on the seabed and get up again and bend over to any angle. The manipulators which try to replace hands are interchangeable according to different tools used.

Oceaneering International bought into the company and obtained the exclusive rights to use *Jim* in the petroleum industry. In 1976 they needed to disentangle a television cable from a drilling structure off the coast of Spain. This was a routine dive but carried *Jim* and his operator to a new world record for 'one at' suits to 439m (1440ft).

A number of versions of *Jims*, 2–13 are now rated by Lloyds for use down to 450m (1500ft) and *Jims* 14 and 15 manufactured by UMEL with a glass fibre body and a large single dome giving hemispherical vision are rated to 600m (2000ft).

These atmospheric systems do depend more than ambient pressure deep diving on having good visibility and are slower than a normal diver in moving and in completing tasks. Once again, human hands and fingers are difficult to replace.

A more recent development, *Wasp*, caters for mid-water diving. Operated by Oceaneering International it is similar to *Jims* 14 and 15 but 'below the waist' it has a cylinder in place of legs. Movement is achieved by using small multi-directional thrusters controlled by foot pedals inside the tube. Another new Oceaneering one atmosphere submersible – *Ocean Arms* 1 – has dived to 866m (2842ft) of Nova Scotia and conducted a well-head inspection. It has a new system of manipulator arms, the operator moving the master control arm whose movements are duplicated by the slave arm outside the bell.

154

Worldwide Diving

The main area of offshore diving is undoubtedly the North Sea, although this will change as time goes by. In 1978 approximately 1500 of the world's estimated 5000 professional deep divers were employed here and Shell Oil were spending $1500 per minute on their operations. Currently the fields off the Shetlands are very important and the area of the Western Approaches is opening up. Production in the North Sea began in the south off Great Yarmouth and some diving contractors still have offices there.

Somewhat shallower diving is carried out in the Middle East and the Gulf of Mexico where many rigs are situated. There is also the Bombay High Field off the Indian Coast and others in Australia and New Zealand. A number of diving operations have also been mounted off Nigeria. Future developments may also occur in the far north, in Labrador and Greenland. The trend is for divers to go deeper and in colder conditions. Comex worked successfully off Labrador at a depth of well over 300m (1000ft).

The Diver

Most of the older divers currently operating offshore in the North Sea have had their basic training in the Royal Navy or the BSAC. Most divers now will have completed one of the government training courses detailed below.

Those taking up deep diving, however, are advised to gain shallow commercial diving experience first. The basic commercial diving courses give the general direction and background, but success will depend on the character, intelligence and motivation of the diver himself. The work as described will consist of bouts of really hard physical work interspersed with long periods of inactivity, all in unpleasant surroundings. The pay is very good but long periods are spent away from home.

Some of the newer deep divers have high educational standards and a high degree of enthusiasm for this exacting type of work. They are generally independent personalities and may have experience in other useful fields such as electronics, pneumatics and hydraulics. The specialist trades of non-destructive tester, fitter, welder and maintenance engineer are always useful besides the diving skills.

Commercial Diver Training Qualifications and Employment

United Kindgom

In the United Kingdom the government's Training Services Division

155

established two standards of basic training – for basic air diving down to 50m (164ft) and for mixed gas deep diving.

A course programme was set up and, besides the Royal Engineers Diving Establishment, three independent diving schools have, to date, been approved to run the scheme. On successful completion by the trainee they may award one of the Training Services' certificates of competence. The three schools are the Underwater Training Centre in Scotland, the Fort Bovisand Underwater Centre in Devon and Prodive Limited in Cornwall.

Although, as already mentioned, there is no substitute for real experience of underwater working, the three months Basic Air Diving and Underwater Working course turns out divers who can work competently down to 50m (164ft) using air with commercial, self-contained, surface demand and free-flow helmet types of equipment. During 'classroom' sessions the trainees learn of the codes of practice, the safety procedures, basic diving physics and physiology and the use of decompression tables. Practical 'wet' sessions involve using all the equipment in sheltered water and open sea, tackling underwater tasks and diving at night in low visibility. These cover the use of underwater communication equipment and of a range of tools.

The course normally includes oxy-arc cutting, rigging, using hydraulic tools, thermal boring, using still photography, television surveying, welding, handling explosives, concreting, gas cutting and it finishes with a task at 40m (130ft) using a hydraulic tool in tidal, low visibility conditions.

Grants

Many trainees have obtained sponsorship from the Government's Training Opportunities Scheme (TOPS) which covers the course fees and accomodation. Others are sponsored by their employers. To be sponsored in this way it is necessary to have a genuine desire to take up a career and it is also necessary to be a fit and competent swimmer. Those taking part in the course must be over 18 years old, and those who have reached 30 must have had previous commercial diving experience. A basic background of secondary education is needed and underwater experience as a sports diver will help, particularly logged experience to British Sub-Aqua Club Second Class Diver Level.

The Training Services Division publishes a number of leaflets on the scheme and the Society for Underwater Technology (SUT) does an excellent booklet on the broader theme of Education and Careers in Underwater Technology. The SUT was founded in 1965 to promote further understanding of the underwater environment and generally to act as the 'learned body' of commercial diving. It aims to further economic and social use of the oceans, help the exchange of information between research workers and technologists, advance the development of techniques and tools and assist the education of scientists and technologists in appropriate disciplines. Meetings and symposia are held on a number of subjects from fish farming to submersibles and membership is open to individuals or companies.

The development of underwater resources in the future will need a whole range of professional skills in science and engineering. Technicians and engineers in particular will be needed. It is thus advisable, if possible, to get a qualification in one of the basic disciplines such as mechanical or chemical engineering or physics. Besides the oil companies, who are the main employers, divers are employed by many industries and organisations manufacturing equipment and providing services from surveying work to the investigation of corrosion.

To enter the industry, professional scientists and engineers should have a good primary degree. Technicians can get basic training in subjects that have a basic marine content. There are a number of courses in underwater technology. These are listed in the *Commonwealth Universities Yearbook* obtainable from most public libraries. Special courses are also available, such as those run by David Baume of the Faculty of Engineering of the North East London Polytechnic. These can lead to a BSc or HND in Mechanical Engineering or Diploma of Higher Education.

School Leavers
Those leaving school should try to get engineering training to fit them for a professional diving career. A list of suitable courses at universities and polytechnics appears in the SUT publication mentioned above. Some possible routes to becoming a diver are shown in Table 3.

Divers are no longer underwater labourers. They are becoming craftsmen, technicians and technologists. They need to be able to stay alive underwater but also to carry out a complex range of tasks. As previously mentioned most commercial divers have been sport divers first and this has provided the basic ability and knowledge which enables them to go underwater safely, maintain equipment and plan dives with a knowledge of diving physics and physiology.

Today these survival skills are becoming more complex in commercial diving. Oxy-helium breathing equipment, heated diving suits and

157

Table 3   ROUTES TO A SUCCESSFUL UK UNDERWATER CAREER

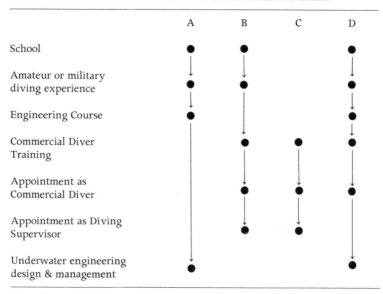

	A	B	C	D
School	●	●		●
Amateur or military diving experience	●	●		●
Engineering Course	●			●
Commercial Diver Training		●	●	●
Appointment as Commercial Diver		●	●	●
Appointment as Diving Supervisor		●	●	
Underwater engineering design & management	●			●

● = "Stops" to obtain qualifications.
Routes A and D provide the best opportunities.

saturation systems require much more technical ability. Modern commercial diving is to sports diving as flying a Concorde is to flying a Tiger Moth.

USA
In the USA there is less government involvement in training. Comprehensive commercial diver training courses are run at specialist schools such as the Commercial Diving Center in California. The schools stress that commercial diving is 'cold, rough and dirty' and involves a lot of competition. Divers may work on a 12 hours on, 12 hours off shift for weeks at a time. They are often the highest paid divers in the world but have to start as a comparatively low paid diver's 'tender' when they have successfully finished their course. Good divers are badly needed in the United States, however, and good opportunities exist for the right calibre of person.

In the USA it is necessary to be between 18 and 32 to take up a diving career. Candidates should have a high school education and be fit for diving. Mechanical skills and, of course, welding experience are much sought after. An air and mixed gas course is recommended and some schools reach 'topside' welding free of charge. A careful comparison should be made between schools and a careful note of the techniques that will actually be taught to students. There is no guarantee of a job to follow the course.

6
The Future

For the amateur, diving is a sport that gives limitless opportunities. After thorough training, the use of the equipment becomes second nature and the diver then decides what to do with the techniques that have been learnt. More and more divers are changing from the 'primitive' pursuits of finding extra food for the table and the acquisition of souvenirs. Courses are available in marine archaeology, biology and photography. The ultimate excitement for an experienced diver is to take part in an expedition – 'diving with a purpose'.

Some of these, such as the Joint Services expedition to Chagos in the Indian ocean have already been mentioned. It is now widely accepted that trained amateur divers can contribute to the scientist's knowledge of undersea life by careful observation. David Bellamy has described amateur divers as 'the eyes under the sea', and US Senator, Lowell Weicker, has stated that; 'The tremendous fund of knowledge represented by sport divers could be harnessed to be extremely valuable to scientists'. The Chagos expedition discovered species that were unknown to science.

So much history is preserved under the sea. In 1979 Graham Campbell, another BSAC member completed a successful film-making expedition to the wreck of the *Royal Oak*, sunk in Scapa Flow during World War 2. Thanet-based divers have discovered the wreck of the 70-gun man o' war *Stirling Castle* sunk in the great storm of 1703 and preserved in amazing condition by the drifting Goodwin Sands.

Today's commercial divers are free from the limitations of restricted air and can be transported to the seabed in vehicles that can also serve as operational bases. What more can we expect? There have been suggestions that man might one day use artifical gills to extract the oxygen from sea water and this forecast was made by Jacques Cousteau at the CMAS World Congress in London in 1962. Researchers are still working in this field.

Professor Kylstra of Duke University in the USA suggested that liquid breathing might be a possibility. Mice lived and breathed successfully with their lungs filled with oxygenated liquid in his experiments. A human volunteer had one lung completely filled with water and reported that he felt no discomfort! Generally it seems more likely that the immediate developments in commercial diving will be in the engineering field.

Underwater cities and industrial complexes of the future have been designed. A sea-bed weekend cottage, the *Galathée* already exists. Undersea farming will combine the new skills of aquaculture and pisciculture and the fish farmer of the future will cultivate the continental shelf at an average depth of 180m (600ft).

The harvesting of the deep sea bed has enormous potential. Millions of 'manganese nodules' lie there ready to be collected for their nickel, copper and cobalt content. Such vessels as the *Glomar Explorer* have been designed for this purpose and hundreds of millions of dollars have been invested to investigate the best methods. The 1970s were described by William Nierenberg, head of the Scripps Institution of Oceanography, as the 'Decade of the Deep', opening a new age of scientific discovery and economic benefit surpassing the returns from the just-ended decade of space exploration. Unfortunately there were economic and political problems.

The long-drawn-out conferences on the Law of the Seabed attempted to decide the boundaries of national interests and who might legally mine the deep oceans. The scientists and engineers waited. Only the industrial countries – Europe, the United States and Japan – have the technological and industrial knowledge and experience to exploit these ocean resources. In 1979 European industry created 'Eurocean' to establish industrial operations in the marine sector through development projects. The projects include thermal energy from the oceans, sea farming, action against oil pollution as well as nodule harvesting. The future is a brilliant one for all those involved under the sea. The underwater adventure is the greatest adventure of the twentieth century, but the exploition of the oceans raises problems of enormous concern. Solutions must and will be found or we will fail in our ambitions and in our destiny.

Appendix
Some Useful Addresses

Sport Diving Organisations

THE WORLD UNDERWATER FEDERATION (CMAS)

    34 rue du Colisée, 75008 Paris, France.

THE BRITISH SUB-AQUA CLUB

    70 Brompton Road, London, SW3 1HA (Free lists of branches & other information available).

BSAC NATIONAL SNORKELLERS CLUB

    (for juniors), 13 Langham Gardens, Wembley, Middlesex HAO 3RG.

NATIONAL ASSOCIATION OF UNDERWATER INSTRUCTORS (NAUI)

    HQ P.O. Box 630, Colton, CA 92324.

NATIONAL YMCA SCUBA HEADQUARTERS

    1611 Candler Building, Atlanta, Georgia 30303.

PROFESSIONAL ASSOCIATION OF DIVING INSTRUCTORS (PADI)

    2064 North Bush Street, Santa Ana, CA 92706.

Photography and Conservation

BRITISH SOCIETY OF UNDERWATER PHOTOGRAPHERS (BSoUP)

    (Current Secretary's address available from BSAC – see above)

UNDERWATER CONSERVATION SOCIETY (UCS)

    Dr. R. Earll, Zoology Dept., University of Manchester, Oxford Road, Manchester M13 9PL.

Scientific Diving and Research

THE UNDERWATER ASSOCIATION FOR SCIENTIFIC RESEARCH LTD.

    c/o Napier Lodge, 46 Monkton Road, Minster-in-Thanet, Kent, CT12 4EB

COMMITTEE FOR NAUTICAL ARCHAEOLOGY

    Sec: Mrs. Margaret Rule FSA, The Roman Palace, Fishbourne, Chichester, Sussex.

THE MARY ROSE TRUST

    Old Bond Store, 48 Warblington Street, Portsmouth, Hants.

THE UNDERSEA MEDICAL SOCIETY

    9650 Rockville Pike, Bathesda, Maryland 20014, USA.

Commercial Diving

THE SOCIETY FOR UNDERWATER TECHNOLOGY (SUT)
    1 Birdcage Walk, London, SW1 9JJ.

Government Recognized Schools

FORT BOVISAND
    Nr Plymouth, Devon, PL9 OAB.
UNDERWATER TRAINING CENTRE
    Inverlochy, Fort William, Highland.
PRODIVE COMMERCIAL TRAINING CENTRE
    Services Area, Falmouth Exploration Base, Falmouth Docks, Cornwall, TR11 4NR.

Journals

THE INTERNATIONAL JOURNAL OF NAUTICAL ARCHAEOLOGY
    Academic Press, 24–28 Oval Road, London, NW1 7DX.
JOURNAL OF UNDERSEA BIOMEDICAL RESEARCH
    Undersea Medical Society, 9650 Rockville Pike, Bathesda, Maryland 20014, USA
JOURNAL OF THE SOCIETY FOR UNDERWATER TECHNOLOGY
    SUT, 1 Birdcage Walk, London, SW1H 9JJ.

Magazines

DIVER
    Magazine of the British Sub-Aqua Club, 40 Grays Inn Road, London, WC1X 8LR.
UNDERWATER WORLD
    Marsh Publications Ltd., 77 Great Peter Street, London, SW1P 2EZ.
SUB-AQUA SCENE
    168 Victoria Street, London, SW1.
SKIN DIVER
    Petersen Publishing Co., 8490 Sunset Blvd, Los Angeles, California 90069.
SPORT DIVER
    Ziff-Davis Publishing Company, One Park Avenue, New York, NY 10016.

A Selected Bibliography

No author covering the history of diving can manage without burrowing and borrowing from the splendid *Deep Diving and Submarine Operations* by Sir Robert Davis (published by his company, Siebe Gorman & Co. and last reprinted in 1969).

I have also found De Latil and Rivoire's excellent *Man and the Underwater World* (Jarrolds, 1956) of great value in assembling the facts especially concerning the development of autonomous equipment.

The third 'pillar of historical wisdom' is James Dugan's *Man Explores the Sea* (Hamish Hamilton, 1956).

Other historical information was gained from Dr. Martin Wells' delightful *You, Me and the Animal World* (Faber, 1964) – Chapter 6 'On Being an Aquatic Man'; from *Seventy Fathoms Deep* and *The Egypt's Gold* both by David Scott (Faber & Faber 1931 and 1932) and from Alexander McKee's *History Under the Sea* (Hutchinson, 1968).

The very beginning of sport diving is described in Guy Gilpatric's *The Compleat Goggler* (The Bodley Head, 1936), and no sport diver should be without Hans Hass' first breathless book *Diving to Adventure* (Jarrolds, 1952) or Cousteau's authoritative *The Silent World* (Hamish Hamilton, 1953).

The exploits of the 'frogmen' are covered in *The Frogmen* by Waldron and Gleeson (Evans, 1952) and in *Above Us The Waves* by Warren and Benson (Harrap, 1953).

The techniques of sport diving will be found in the British Sub Aqua Club's *Diving Manual* (latest edition, 1979) and information on other sports organisations around the world was obtained from the World Underwater Federation's *International Yearbook of the Underwater World* (Aquatica – 3rd edition, 1975). Those interested in the *Mary Rose* should search out a copy of *King Henry VIII's Mary Rose* by Alexander McKee (Souvenir Press, 1973), and those wanting a general survey of underwater archaeology are referred to Keith Muckelroy's *Maritime Archaeology* and *Archaeology Underwater* (Cambridge University Press, 1978, and McGraw Hill, 1980).

The 'underwater' books of the pioneer naturalist, William Beebe are worth searching for. Besides *Half Mile Down* (The Bodley Head, 1935) they include *Nonsuch Island, Beneath Tropic Seas* and *The Arcturus Adventure*. Modern diving science is covered in *Progress in Underwater Science* (The proceedings of the symposia of The Underwater Association) published annually by Pentech Press, and some earlier work will be found in *Underwater Science* by Woods and Lythgoe (OUP, 1971).

Perhaps the best known book on commercial diving techniques is *Commercial Oilfield Diving* by Zinkowski.

Finally, those interested in guides to marine life from the diver's point of view are referred to:

The Hamlyn Guide to the Seashore and Shallow Seas of Britain and Europe, by Campbell (Hamlyn, 1976).

A Field Guide to the Mediterranean Sea Shore, by Luther and Fiedler (Collins, 1976).

Fishes of the Sea (*British Isles, N. Europe and Mediterranean*), by John & Gillian Lythgoe (Blandford, 1971).

Coral Reef Fishes of the Indian and West Pacific Oceans, by Carcasson (Collins, 1977) and

Marine Life (*An illustrated Encyclopedia of the Invertebrates in the Sea*), by David and Jennifer George (Harrap, 1979).

Index

*The figures in **bold** refer to colour plates. Those in italics refer to the page numbers of black and white illustrations. Other figures refer to text pages.*